The Imperfect Logic of the Heart

Codependency, Empathy, Love

A Memoir

By Richard Schwachter

Table of Contents

MUCH LATER 6

CHAPTER 1: 1954 10

CHAPTER 2: THE NEW SCHOOL 1957........................ 24

CHAPTER 3: WISCONSIN 1962.....................................33

CHAPTER 4: CLEVELAND 1969.................................... 46

CHAPTER 5: EPIPHANY/IRIE.. 60

CHAPTER 6: EARLY 80'S.. 63

CHAPTER 7: MANHATTAN.. 70

CHAPTER 8: LOS ANGELES 79

CHAPTER 9: BACK TO CLEVELAND............................ 98

CHAPTER 10 MEET TAMMA 108

CHAPTER 11: FLORIDA 122

CHAPTER 12: BLEEDER.. 133

CHAPTER 13: WEST PALM BEACH 145

CHAPTER 14: JAYNE 157

CHAPTER 15: POMPANO BEACH............................... 166

CHAPTER 16: WESTIN FLORIDA 180

CHAPTER 17: BARBARA: CALIFORNIA..................... 187

CHAPTER 18: WHAT'S IT ALL ABOUT?..................... 193

My Turn

I stuffed my issues under my pillow
For review in a black and white
Dream show; while in blazing sunlight
I toiled at yours.
Distractions of Bach partitas kept
My demons at bay;
Their shouts muted in organ aural waves;
Yet for yours there was focus
And clarity;
Solutions (mine for you
Not yours for you) dancing
With octave changes
and plucked strings.
And there was that mirror
Reflecting an image unknown
To me.
That man who one day
I would meet.
Who would catch my eye
And hold me with his love
And answers.
Assure me
In silence that it was
My turn.

MUCH LATER

HER ROOM LOOKED like a hotel room at Circus Circus after a week of gambling and drinking. There were multiple ash trays that were no longer "cleanable"; doggie bags that may or may not contain edible substances; folded aluminum foil balls that contained either the remnants of ash from her precious crack pipe or just plain cigarette ash. Somehow she knows the difference. And then there were slippers and robes that may be for warm or cold weather or more likely for pre or post hangover and of course vodka bottles. When she was a beginner they were classy bottles and brands like Stoli, Grey Goose and Belvedere. Now they were store brands or worse, like a jug bottle of Costco.

Nothing was hung but rather arranged in piles based on utility. A pile for stepping out of the shower. A pile for having to go downstairs to the kitchen. A pile for vehicle travel without leaving the vehicle and a pile for vehicle travel when you have to leave the vehicle. This last pile essentially just added a jacket.

There were things to make her nails look less like the ruined, cracked remnants they were. And then there were the bed toys. The thing you see advertised late night: a vibrating back rest so you can sit up in bed and watch TV while you die from cigarette smoke. The cigarette smoke is winning its battle over the overpriced Sharper Image Air Cleaner. A four hundred dollar lie. And of course along with the smoke comes the ubiquitous cigarette burns. These marked yellow and brown trails randomly spot the cheap but new carpet and even test the rubber backed mattress cover. Is there a more fragrant violation of my lease terms than these burn marks in my smoke- free apartment?

6

She had the windows closed and the air conditioner off.

"I know it's a little stuffy in here, but I can't stand to hear the ambulances. The Delray Beach geriatric ambulance club. Free Medicare ride to the hospital and always when I'm trying to sleep."

"Did they get it right?"

"Two orders of Beef Yegamachi. Tora?"

"I hope you didn't tip them. Those assholes?"

"You'd think after all the money I've given them that they wouldn't give me a hard time. So I slurred a little in their precious restaurant. Fuck them!"

"I didn't try to order a drink."

"I was just waiting for their overpriced Jap food."

"If they don't want me in the place they should deliver."

This familiar rant barks from a mouth parked parallel to a king sized Westin Hotel pillow attached to a slender t-shirted female frame reclined on a king-sized pillow-top Sealy. It's not the W but her apartment in Delray Beach. Actually my apartment. Our sixth in seven years. I've moved out.

"Anyway, THANK YOU."

"You didn't have to drive over to pick it up. But I wasn't going to wait there and let them continue to humiliate me."

"FUCK THEM."

"Have you eaten?"

"Yes, dear, it's 10PM. I ate at 6."

"It's 10? Ok then." She seems to be corresponding with someone. There are small legal pads everywhere with notes and lists and still larger pads with block letters reminiscent of a serial killer's note to the newspaper announcing his next victim.

Pill bottles are everywhere. Some with names ending in "azapam" for fun and others which are supposed to help her bipolar condition. So says Doctor New Black Lexus Convertible who would write a nun a prescription for heroin if asked.

And there I stand, Mr. Codependent, barely taking it all in because it is now so familiar.

CHAPTER 1: 1954

I NEVER READ PROUST but somehow I remember the magical "madeleine cookie." If you dipped it in a cup of tea it evoked your childhood memories. A disinfectant used at a subway stop in New York City had the same effect on me. Apparently it was the identical compound that cleaned the floors of my elementary school in Cleveland, Ohio. Its scent sent me back in time. A journey I warmly welcomed this late in life. My 73-year-old brain cells can become invaded at any time by beta-amyloid sticky stuff that will make the trip impossible. Even now, I confess, my brain may have rewritten some of the facts to make them more palatable and relatable.

I was eight years old when I was sentenced to the hall floor waiting for my mother summoned by the authorities to rescue me. It would only take her a sidewalk stroll of ten houses to my school to hear Principal Berger describe his latest disappointment with one of her sons.

When she arrived, I watched her shoes circle her prey while his shuffled sideways. When I dared look up I thought I saw more fear in Mr. Berger's eyes than my own. His eyes darting from me to my mom's face, strangely, by way of her legs strapped into high heel shoes.

"No, it's not Larry, it's Richard." Berger expressed surprise.

"Apparently Richard threw a bit of a tantrum today learning he was one A short of winning baseball tickets for a straight "A" report card."

My mother never bothered to look at me before she responded:

"That is surprising…a tantrum for one A missing."

"Which one was missing?"

"Well, I'm not sure that's relevant." Berger frowns. I remember now he had one of the first "comb-over" hair treatments I had ever witnessed. Even then I knew something was not quite aesthetically correct.

"Well apparently it was relevant to Richard."

Mom looks at me for the first time. I think I remember a wink.

"Ok…it was handwriting."

"Well of course he was upset. He's left handed like his father and you don't supply left handed school desks…so shame on Groveland Elementary. You need to judge his handwriting based on a lefty trying to write on a righty desk. By that standard he should have received an A plus."

"You need to change his grade!"

Our address, 4337 Groveland Road, University Heights, Ohio, zipcode 18, sprouted from the once vacant suburban woods and reflected the magical rebirth of American spirit following WWII. People were moving to the suburbs with new ambition and GI loan borrowing power. Our $9,000 box looked like all the other neighbors' homes, but there was still excitement and pride of ownership in the air. I was ten years old in 1954 and it was a glamorous, exciting time. There was Ian Fleming's "Live and Let die." Marilyn had married Joe. We liked IKE and of course there was Brown v. Board of Education and "Duck and Cover." There were no telephone Area Codes. Our exchange was "Evergreen." We had a milk man, a bread man, ice cream man, pretzel potato chip man and we actually liked, not feared, the policeman who knew our name and our parents' names.

If there was an end of segregation in schools, our middle class ghetto still housed many girls with names like Clara and Oprah living in the attic of our tract houses, operating the mangle iron in the basement and cooking their own childhood dishes like fried chicken and potato salad.

Our houses were all laid out in rows with little differences between them. "Little pink house for you and me." If I lifted my bedroom window at night, my neighbor Mary could read me a nighttime story if my mother had more pressing duties. My most precious possessions were my Schwinn bike and my Emerson clock radio. The bike allowed freedom while the clock radio was succor to loneliness.

Were my codependent training wheels beginning with my brother Larry?

In '54, there was a lot to watch on TV. Our house had one of the first TV's on the block. We had one in the "family room" (what once was the screened in porch) and one in my parents' bedroom. We watched Lassie, Father knows Best, Rin Tin Tin, and of course I Love Lucy. If our parents were gone there were Swanson TV dinners with turkey pieces, cornbread, mashed potatoes and peas and TV Time popcorn (with the corn on one side and the grease on the other). Dessert was from the Good Humor ice cream man or Sealtest vanilla ice cream and Dad's Root beer.

Larry and I each had our own RCA Victor record players that only played 45's (smaller records with a big hole in the center), which we stacked by the players as prized possessions. You did not touch dad's turntable or amplifier which played only LP's, also forbidden without permission. I had in my collection: "Oh My Papa" and "Mr. Sandman." Larry had "Rock Around the Clock" and other more obscure "Negro" records. Dad listened to Frank Sinatra and Peggy Lee.

Dad's souped- up stereo was in the basement. He preferred the large tape deck to vinyl and often listened with his new Ampex headphones that shut out any household noise that could interrupt his concentration on the amazing stereo "separation." I listened in my

12

room, reading comic books. Mom talked on the phone while she knitted and chewed Dentine gum. Larry sat on his bed with legs on the floor and bounced to the music until, after years of this behavior, he had created a depression wave in the bed.

Looking back now, I wonder if Larry was autistic or had some form of Asperger's. I do know he was dyslexic and answered to only himself.

The war between my father and Larry began shortly after Larry's first IQ test, which put him at a near-genius level. How could someone with such a high level of intelligence do so poorly at school? To my father it was lack of effort. To Larry it was probably lack of interest.

My father, Robert Sheldon Schwachter, was born in coal country Williamson, West Virginia not far from Jackson, Kentucky of "Hillbilly Elegy" fame. His father Harry was not a coal miner or a traditional hillbilly. His shovel work was selling ladies clothing to a captive audience of coal miners' wives. Harry had moved up in the world by marrying the boss's daughter. He was a runaway from Hungary and his studious but unemployed Orthodox Jewish father. A stowaway on a cruise ship en route to America. Once discovered, he danced for the passengers for pennies. Somehow he arrived on the Ohio River. When the boat stopped in Cincinnati, he randomly got off and eventually got a job as a window dresser. He courted and finally married the store owner's daughter, my great great grandfather, Papa Brown's daughter, Rose Brown. A Jewish girl from a pre-Civil War family.

Harry was sent to Williamson to open a branch store where he succeeded and ultimately owned most of the town's assets. He accomplished this by hard work and a remarkable ability to not only know everyone's name but also their business. He was the towns entertainer and storyteller. He could recite almost all of the Rubaiyat of Omar Khayyam and later paid me handsomely for every passage I could memorize. (I still have a few stuck in my brain.) One in particular seems particularly relevant now:

13

"I sent my Soul through the Invisible,
Some letter of that After-life to spell:
And by and by my Soul return'd to me,
And answer'd: 'I Myself am Heav'n and Hell"

Rose was the best cook in the state, sharing her bounty with any family temporarily in need.

Harry had three children: a boy, Bob, (my father) and two daughters, Mary Lou and Betty. Bob looked like Jeff Chandler of movie fame with dark hair and striking blue eyes. A swimmer's body and a natural born leader personality. Charisma was his greatest gift.

Dad was off to West Virginia State with his Catholic girlfriend until his mother Rose announced that he was going solo to Ohio State or remaining in his room for the rest of his life.

He excelled at Ohio State becoming, president of the student body, president of his fraternity, and Jayne's new husband. The latter achievement was easy since Jayne lassoed him. And he could not believe his luck since she was gorgeous, sassy, rich, and had her own car with her name etched on the side. He spruced up his image with speech classes and the finer touches of manners, but those extras probably weren't necessary since by some estimates Bob had it all.

Jayne Deutsch was Cleveland Jewish royalty. Her father was the only Jewish funeral director in Cleveland and one of the oldest Jewish families in this steel town. Her grandfather on her father's side had been a carriage maker with an office where Cleveland's Terminal Tower now stood. Jayne's mother Rose was also a Deutsch. No need to change her name at marriage. Her Austrian and later New York family were the jewelers of choice for many years in Cleveland. Jayne's mother, my Meme Rose, was highly educated and expected the same of her children. Her older son ultimately complied by getting a degree from Case, the MIT of the Midwest. Jayne didn't need a degree. She had natural blond hair and blue eyes, great legs and a sharp wit. But as those that underestimated her soon discovered, she also possessed a

14

special brand of intelligence. Jayne excelled at knowing the difference between shit and shinolla a quality not fully infused into Robert's otherwise complete package.

Harry had a job for my father. He had in fact bought him a men's clothing store in Williamson. If his son wanted to get married he had to leave school with only one quarter left at Ohio State before his degree was achieved and move to W.VA. to open the Roberts- Morris men's clothing store.

Without considering the consequences, mom and dad jumped at the opportunity which lasted long enough for Larry to be born and my dad to realize that my mom was not a West Virginia girl and that Cleveland offered a brighter future for their new family. Five years later with a lot of extra physical activity (which my mother loved to brag about) I was finally conceived and born in Cleveland. My father eventually got his degree from Ohio State when he was over 60 years old. Accepting the degree with cap and gown was one of my father's proudest moments.

In 1944, my Mom was living in Cleveland with her parents while my Dad was preparing to be a "frog man" at the Great Lakes training facility in Chicago. Fortunately the war ended before he got in the water and we were all able to move to suburbia in a newly built house in a newly built world financed by the GI Bill.

My Dad's new career would be on the sales floor at the Deutsch's jewelry store. No dead bodies for him at the mortuary, although this alternative was offered. He'd go with the other Deutsch.

He excelled at this new job with his great looks and personality until a representative from Dunn and Bradstreet visited the store and wanted some basic information for their updated report. My Dad was asked his title. He proudly responded Vice President. D&B asked him: "Which one?" Apparently everyone working the floor in the store was a VP. This did not sit well with my Dad and he stormed out to become his own man. He would become a wholesale diamond salesman on the road.

Dad traveled the small cities in Ohio and Pennsylvania with a suitcase filled with diamonds in the trunk of his car and his German Luger strapped to his chest. Every small town had a local jewelry store and these stores became my dad's clients. He usually left on his diamond route early Monday morning and returned late Friday afternoon. There were no turnpikes so it was back roads and small hotels that had a safe. Phone calls were expensive so the person to person trick was employed. The phone would ring and the operator would say:

"You have a person-to-person phone call from Sheldon Schwachter for Harry Schwachter…will you accept the charges?"

If it was my dad you would say:

"Sorry, Harry Schwachter is not in."

And then a few minutes later my dad would call back station-to-station without the operator at a lesser charge.

Beating the phone company was something Larry taught me. If you carried a thumb tack in your wallet, you could stick it through the exposed wire that led from the pay phone to the headset, ground it on the coin return, and get an immediate dial tone for free.

Dad's travel requirements affected the dynamics of our household in ways that profoundly affected the remainder of my life. While my dad was gone the full Oedipus complex was in effect for the brother-mother relationship: in Freudian theory *"the complex of emotions aroused in a young child by an unconscious sexual desire for the parent of the opposite sex and a wish to exclude the parent of the same sex."*

While my dad was gone my brother pretended to be the man of the house. In effect he was. Discipline was not my mother's strong suit and Larry was too beautiful and clever to sustain anger in my mom

16

for long periods of time. She once tried to spank him with a hair brush that broke in two, prompting laughter on both their parts. And Larry lived his life his own way. And in fact did so until he died.

One Sunday Larry accompanied his little brother to downtown Cleveland's Euclid Avenue Temple for Sunday school. As the 32 B Heights Express bus stopped at the temple my brother reminded me that directly across the street from the temple was the best donut and chocolate cookie store in Cleveland. The option was not "let's get a cookie when Temple is over. It was: "COOKIE or TEMPLE…TEMPLE or COOKIE."

We would get a cookie, go visit my great uncle at the jewelry store, visit Record Rendezvous, and then catch the appropriate bus back home where I would be complicit in my brothers lies, out of guilt not fear, since Larry never was unkind to me.

One time we did get caught. Uncle Jake or the Gene Carroll show was a Cleveland TV show popular in the 50's. My dad wrote some advertising copy for the show and produced a children's record that was an early version of the Chipmunk gimmick. Gene would record voices and then speed them up to create the effect for Johnny the Mud Turtle and Suzy the Squirrel dad's idea. One of the sponsors of the children's show was Spang Glazed Donuts. My brother convinced me one Sunday to skip temple and go to the live show. Gene knew me from my dad and our visits to his farm and knew it would be safe to bring me on stage for the live commercial. I would bite into a donut and express my complete delight on live TV. What happened instead was I bit into the donut and lost one of my teeth on live TV. My parents didn't see the show but did hear about the incident from an amused Gene Carroll.

When my dad returned on Fridays late afternoon he would say hello to me before I was shipped out to my grandparents until Sunday. After dinner out with my grandparents at one of the two same restaurants every week (Chinese food or ribs), I would return home and the cycle would begin again. I did not spend much time with my

17

dad and when the family was all together the elephant in the room was always Larry's aberrant behavior. When the entire family was together the Larry-dad fight would begin again over Larry's misadventures while my dad was gone. At the peak of the anger I would retreat to my room and wonder why my dad seemed to hate Larry when I adored him.

When my dad was gone I was lonely during the week, particularly at bed time. Homework done, I would turn the timer on the clock radio to 30 minutes and look for something to listen to to send me to sleep. (I have never been able to fall asleep without conversation in the room.) I remember listening to Ozzy and Harriet and my favorite the Lone Ranger to send me to my dreams.

My grandfather was in kidney failure before a dialysis machine had been invented. My grandmother, with a little help, cared for him. He sat mostly in his large green vinyl arm chair or in bed. On occasion he was outside looking at his beautiful garden and creeping bent grass. The carpet-like lawn required a special Jacobsen lawn motor. His gardener, Mr. Portero, would supply me with a ready supply of strawberries when in season and eventually allowed me to grow my own patch which, when ripe I would stuff in my pocket for my bike ride home.

Friday nights at my grandparents we watched Your Hit Parade and I Remember Mama and we talked. My grandmother was a fanatical sports fan. Her brother was the first owner of the Cleveland Browns (originally a baseball franchise). She scored every pitch in every game the Cleveland Indians played. I did not share her enthusiasm. Her neighbor's son Mike was my age and I loved his company, but he too was a sports fanatic and I had to pretend to be interested in his baseball card collection.

Actually what interested me was the news and God. My grandfather read the three Cleveland papers every day: the News, the Plain Dealer and the Press. (He explained that the word news also stood for north, east, south and west.) We listened to John Cameron Swazey for national news and Dorothy Fuldheim for local.

My interest in the news started with my grandparents' friends. When they were around they didn't send me to "go play" but instead included me in their conversations. No one had ever before asked me what I thought about anything. They did. And I wanted to be able to answer them and participate in the conversation.

I think because my grandfather was dying and was also an undertaker and I had actually seen dead bodies at the funeral home (because Larry had forced me to look), I was a little over-obsessed with death and dying and religion. My grandmother believed religion was all nonsense and theater but she wanted me to have an open mind. She had read all of Will and Ariel Durant and allowed me to read a little of one volume, which explained how religions were an outgrowth of the seasons: the winter solstice for Christmas and the spring solstice for Easter. Praying to the idols who allowed the sun to return so there would again be food. How the Jews needed one God that traveled because they were shepherds and couldn't carry their dead with them. I learned that most of the world didn't believe in Judaism. I couldn't understand the trinity idea at all. I still don't.

I remember the strange sight of false teeth next to a glass at night and my grandmother's ruined feet. Her mother had told her that pretty girls do not have feet larger than size four. Grandmother's were size 6 so apparently her feet were force fed into shoes too small as a child. But mostly I remember being treated like a whole person not just a little boy. Someone who had things to say and opinions and someone who responded to love and respect.

When my grandmother asked me to help her change my grandfather's soiled bed she made no apology for his illness and expected me to understand what happens as we age and decay. I can't think of anyone I loved more than Meme Rose.

Meanwhile the wars between my brother and father were escalating. As my brother continued to fail at school, he had strangely developed skills that astonished my father and made him all the more angry. Television was the new phenomenon. We had an early one and everybody wanted one. Strangely Larry could fix anyone's broken TV or radio or for that matter anyone's broken anything. He wouldn't read a history book but studied Popular Electronics and Popular Mechanics as if they were the holy grail.

And then my brother announced that he wanted to be a shortwave operator. A neighbor had a shortwave receiver but my brother wanted more. Somehow a shortwave set appeared in the house. I think Uncle Sid my mother's brother got bored with his own set and gave it to Larry who after a few weeks learned the Morse code and became the youngest ham radio operator in Ohio.

Now my father was even more confused and convinced that Larry just didn't care about what was important. Where was the discipline for school? And so the war continued. Meanwhile the "good child" got all A's and starred in children's theater. Never complained. Was almost too quiet.

I knew I was not in my brother's league; he was brilliant and I was, if you looked closely, ordinary. I also knew Larry didn't care a bit about my father's judgment of his behavior. He was his own judge and jury and quite comfortable with his own assessment. The world adored him partly because they sensed he didn't need their adoration.

The good child was fooling the world with hard work as opposed to raw talent. Misjudged by my parents. Put on a pedestal I didn't want. Not being comfortable to fail or be less than exceptional. Alone. Feeling the need to mediate, to somehow help my brother and explain him to my parents. One thing for sure: I would not add to their problems by being a problem. The golden boy would never disappoint.

Maybe sensing my distress, my parents arranged to send me to overnight summer camp for eight weeks. "He needs to get out of this house for the summer." I was ten years old and had never been away from home for more than two nights. I had never played baseball, cared nothing for sports, had an early near drowning experience and was terrified of the water, and needed noise to fall asleep.

Camp Roosevelt in Perry, Ohio had a history that dated back to Theodore Roosevelt and the Rough Riders. I didn't know much about that history except that older campers would write their names on the cabin walls and sign them with their years of attendance. My uncle's name was on the wall and other names dating back, I guessed, to Teddy.

My first night in our cabin was unsettling to begin with but not helped by watching our camp counselor Marshall Glickman remove his wooden leg and put a sock over his stump. He had several legs and one special one for the water.

The first day we were introduced to the "camp letter." This was what we were all supposed to be working towards achieving by the end of the summer. The letter had sections like scouting, nature, work hours, craft, etc. For example, if you could start a camp fire with three matches you could earn some of your scouting points. Every day we would head off to work on the letter. Getting the letter early in the year was considered a very prestigious achievement. New campers did not get early letters. But I was concerned that I had to be successful at camp, like I was successful at school to maintain the balance in the Schwachter household. Once again I would balance out Larry.

The previous year Larry had been sent to Camp Conestoga, a much more prestigious camp than Roosevelt. The first week they had an overnight hike where you sleep in the woods in a sleeping bag. In the morning Larry was no longer there. He was picked up by the police 70 miles away. He had one successful hitch and then a truck driver called the police. With the help of a seasoned Camp Roosevelt professional camper a few weeks older than I, we managed the first and second letters in camp, an amazing achievement at the time. I knew my parents would be proud. At least my dad.

My mother was getting weary of my over achievements.

I learned at Camp that I had athletic abilities. I was very fast and strong. I discovered baseball. I was a lousy fielder, had never played catch with my dad or Little League, but I was a great hitter. I was a home run guy and at first base I didn't have to judge a fly ball. Peer pressure finally taught me to swim and I quickly excelled at it.

Except for the camp haircut,0 which made my mother furious because it was so short, my camp adventure was successful. But did I have as much fun as I could have if I weren't worried about the damn camp letter, if I weren't obsessed with maintaining my status as golden boy?

Letters from home only hinted at a new crisis. What was going on with Larry?

CHAPTER 2: THE NEW SCHOOL 1957

WHEN YOU GET TO BE MY AGE you watch your body slowly fall apart. In my sixties I replaced both cataract clouded lenses, stitched up the back of my eye that had collapsed with a scleral buckle and bought my first pair of orthotics. Now in my seventies I am looking forward to buying a new knee and possibly if I can afford it new teeth. All this decay happened slowly.

Puberty, on the other hand struck like lightning. One day you're reading Batman and the next you're peeking at Playboy. A shocking emission from my enhanced penis happened at the same time that I grew four inches in height, developed a minus eight refractive error and a raging case of acne. If these extreme alterations in my physical self were not disturbing enough, my mother's announcement that I would be starting a new junior high school, in a new neighborhood, away from all my friends, sent my already-raging hormonal imbalance into overdrive.

I certainly was not going to win over new friends with my grotesque new physical self and Shaker Heights, my new neighborhood, was horrifying. Only rich people lived there.

Shaker Heights was conceived in the early 1900's by the Van Sweringen Brothers (Oris and Mantis), railroad billionaires. Their idea was to plan a community where both the design of the houses and the type of people allowed to live there would be strictly controlled. These restrictions were put in place in order to maintain Shaker's "spatial and social distinctiveness" and contrast with the big city life in downtown Cleveland. In other words, only rich people need apply and hopefully only highly educated white rich people.

Lyman Boulevard, was the site of our new home, the last street in Shaker on its far east side, the furthest away from Shaker Heights High

School. Construction would be finished the summer before school was to start. We were not rich. Dad's jewelry trips did not suddenly get lucrative. Actually his small jewelry store customers were all going broke as the malls and chain stores eclipsed their fading business with larger inventories and better prices. My dad was also going broke. My mother was not. The land and money for the new house came from my grandfather Deutsch. Some of the cash was money my mother had saved, but the land was bought years before by my grandfather. Actually my dad was now in the property management business, managing a building in downtown Cleveland owned by his attorney.

There was a new crisis with my brother. My mother was at war with the high school dean who decided at the last minute that Larry needed to go to summer school if he was to get a high school diploma. Larry thought he was graduating with his class but apparently his frequent absenteeism had caught up with him and what had been a D now had morphed into an F. Apparently some sort of compromise had been reached, which was fortunate because my parents were planning to send Larry to Wooster Junior College in Wooster Mass where he could get tuned up to go to a "real college." Shaker was probably happy to get rid of Larry.

Years later, I told my Mother a story about the dean she hated who had bullied all the kids, some of the teachers, and even some of the parents. One of our teachers at Shaker, who worked there while the dean was in full abuse, also worked as a travel guide in the summers. Returning from one of his trips he sat next to an amusing man on his flight who made Liberace look like John Wayne. In a casual conversation he asked our teacher friend what he did. Our friend responded that he was a teacher at Shaker Heights High School. The very gay seat mate responded:

"Oh my god. My boyfriend is the dean there."

That information was the weapon our friend used during his teaching career to escape the bully dean.

25

"Hey, I met a friend of yours on a long plane ride."

Larry never stayed at Wooster for more than a few days. A long story can be abridged by fast forwarding to the end when my mom discovered that Larry had pulled a Camp Conestoga. After saying a goodbye to my parents, Larry bolted and made his way to Ohio State in Columbus where he stayed with a friend and worked in a deli. Mail from my parents to Wooster was being forwarded to Larry so it took a little time to discover that Larry had never gone to a single class at Wooster. This was going to be a hard one for me to balance out. You had better behave in Shaker. Be an extra good boy.

To help ease my transition and hopefully introduce me to some future Shaker friends my mother enrolled me in the Florence Shapiro Dancing School. Florence and her spinster sister Hattie would have named it the "Shaker Finishing School" if they could have gotten away with it. There was a little bit of dance instruction and a lot of pomp and circumstance for the fancy Shaker Jewish community. Everyone entered the ballroom as couples, arranged by height, with the girls wearing white gloves and the boys their new suits. None of the popular dances were taught. The classics were in control: the waltz, the tango, the box step to the music of Hattie at the piano. Definitely no mambo or cha cha.

Florence knew about my dancing reputation and made sure I followed the routine. By the time I started Florence Shapiro I was kind of a seasoned professional. mambo and cha cha were the rage among the adults that took dance lessons from Carlos and Kay or Tony and Yolanda. My parents had arranged private lessons with their friends in our basement on Groveland. I had learned the steps when I was a little boy watching from the basement steps while my parents' friends were taught. Sometimes I was allowed to participate when the teachers would say in frustration "look, even Richie can do this…it's not hard."

A few years later I had taken more lessons from Carlos and Kay and was part of their advanced class that on occasion performed at the Bar Mitzvahs and country clubs in the area. There were also weekend and temple dances. I was such a frequent winner in these contests that eventually I was not allowed to enter. People knew me as the guy who danced. That was all they knew but it was my ticket to a few new friends at Shaker.

At Florence's famous costume party, I came dressed as a girl. Not an unusual thing to do back in the early sixties before the LGBT community. Florence asked me to get my mother.

"Dear, you can't be here without a costume."

I quickly straightened her out. Another one of those Florence Shapiro events, the Hayride, introduced me to my junior high, high school and beyond, girlfriend and future mother of my children. The famous Dr. Jac Geller's middle child Betsy.

Construction had not been completed on the new junior high school I was to attend in seventh grade, so the school district arranged for half-day classes at the old junior high until the new facility was finished. My half day was in the afternoon so our mornings were free. Those mornings became ice skating events with most of my new junior high class. My English teacher's new husband owned the rink. Lots of fun but little learning taking place.

In a blink of an eye junior high school sped into senior high school as my confidence and respect for my intelligence eroded year by year. There were several factors at work beyond the normal distress my peers faced on the way to adulthood.

There was Betsy.

There was Larry.

There was Latin.

There was the Ivy League.

If I had some recognition as "the dancer" I ultimately became known as Betsy's boyfriend. A Jewish cheerleader was an oxymoron.

27

Yet Betsy was Byron and then Shaker's cheerleader and we were attached at the hip. This relationship was a mystery to most who considered me clearly unworthy of the beautiful Miss Personality. But like most complicated relationships there was more to it than first appearances. I had a confusing set of unresolved issues in my family dynamic and Betsy had her own.

If I couldn't resolve mine at home, somehow in my youthful ignorance I thought I would be more effective with Betsy's own entanglements. Hers were classic. She was the middle child who got all the attention from everyone but her mother, who seemed to be compensating to bolster the fortunes of her less blessed sisters. She got little from her father, who had delegated raising the girls to his wife while he hid in the hospital, an environment he understood far better than his home. My role was simple. Shut up and listen. We became "relationship addicted." Something I never fully understood until many years later when I first learned about codependency.

Larry's situation at home became even more complicated by his illness. In the short time following his aborted college experience Larry had found employment and a wife. His few week marriage ended in an annulment following his serious colitis condition that almost killed him. My first airplane ride was to fly to Cincinnati where he was living and drive his car home while he recovered. Larry moved back into our new house and started to recover by gaining a little weight. He had been reduced to the size of an Auschwitz survivor. Our diet at home now included those foods prescribed for him by his doctor who we would later discover was incompetent. We ate a lot of calves liver and drank an enormous amount of ice tea.

If I was an all A student during my primary grades, those former skills seemed to have eluded me in my new schools. Part of the problem started early on when I lost the ability to listen in class. This was not the result of normal distractions that accompany a teenager but a more extreme condition. I literally saw lips moving and nothing coming out. My hearing was fine but the words made no sense and if

I was to learn anything it would have to be at home from a book. There might be a name for this condition but the resolution of the problem did not fully occur until college. Even when I went to the movies I was unable to follow the story. Strange.

I was a hopeless Latin student, although today I love to recite from memory the first few lines of Virgil's Aeneid:

> *Arma virumque cano, Troiae qui primus ab oris*
> *Italiam, fato profugus, Laviniaque venit*
> *litora, multum ille et terris iactatus et alto*
> *vi superum saevae memorem Iunonis ob iram;*
> *multa quoque et bello passus, dum conderet urbem,*   5
> *inferretque deos Latio, genus unde Latinum,*
> *Albanique patres, atque altae moenia Romae*

Arms I sing and the man who first from the coasts of Troy, exiled by fate, came to Italy and Lavinian shores; much buffeted on sea and land by violence from above, through cruel Juno's unforgiving wrath, and much enduring in war also, till he should build a city and bring his gods to Latium; whence came the Latin race, the lords of Alba, and the walls of lofty Rome.

My Dad encouraged me to take Latin, assuring me that it would help in developing my English vocabulary. If you took it in 9th grade you had to continue in 10th. And I was advised that you needed three years of a language to get into a decent college, so you took it in 11th as well. From the beginning, I never got Latin and my lack of ability continued to escalate until I was hopelessly behind. In my third year with the wonderful Mr. Strater, I watched my genius classmates play with the Latin sections creating modern translations in iambic pentameter worthy of new classic offerings while I stared at the Latin page and feared being called on once again to embarrass myself in front of the class.

Strater loved to stretch a rubber band around his forehead and play with it while you watched in apprehension of it snapping. But it never did. He called me into his office after class towards the end of the semester.

"Doctor Schwachter, you are failing my class! But I have failed you as well. I have checked your records and actually talked to your other teachers and I know you have the ability to get an A and yet you are falling close to the fearful F. What has happened here is a failure on both our parts. We should have offered succor earlier. Special help, extra help, extraordinary help to prop you up. But now doctor, I fear it is too late so I am offering you a life raft, an alternative to failure. As of this day you are to become the Virgil scholar of our class. You will know everything about the Aeneid and everything about Virgil. I will only call on you in class with reference to these subjects. I will never ask you to translate. If you can perform these functions satisfactorily as our Virgil scholar you will pass this class. I cannot, however, assure you of much more than a D. But then you will understand. Yes, doctor? Okay doctor Schwachter?"

I fared much better in my other classes and had a good but lopsided result on my SAT's. Extremely good on the English part, not as good on the math. My grandmother's insistence that the dictionary be frequently consulted had worked its magic on my vocabulary.

My class was filled with brilliant children. Obviously Shaker parents offered a great gene pool but by any standard the class was extraordinary. If I was uncertain then, the years have confirmed my assessment by producing extraordinary professional people. Everyone in our class went to college and of course the Ivy League was a big deal then as now. For some reason my high school guidance counselor thought Colgate, a lesser Ivy League school would be a good fit.

I had labored hard and long on Shaker's swim team never achieving a school letter. My breast stroke skills were quite good but not better than the number one and two in the state who were also on Shaker's team. I was in the top ten in the state but not good enough to start for Shaker. That was unlucky but swimming was a sport I enjoyed. One of the few you could "play" if you were extremely nearsighted. Contact lenses were not around yet. You didn't need to see much in the pool. And as long as I was on the swim team I didn't have to take gym.

My guidance teacher must have thought of Colgate because he knew they liked swimmers. I visited Colgate with a friend who ultimately enrolled there and swam on the team. I hated every moment of my visit to Colgate in Hamilton, New York including the Nazi children who were on the swim team. One of these charming children later knocked out the front teeth of one of my oldest friends who left that school and transferred to Ohio State.

Still in the hunt for a college, my dad and I went on a road trip to Chicago to see Northwestern. The vibe was not there for me (the city frankly scared me) so I asked my dad if we could go another few hours north to Madison. One of my Roosevelt counselors was a student there and loved it.

Wisconsin in the summer is particularly beautiful. I had one look at Lake Mendota and knew this would be my college. We checked into the Edgewater Hotel on the lake and ended up having dinner the first night with a woman and her son from Milwaukee who were checking things out. My dad and the extremely attractive woman seemed to be enjoying a harmless flirtation while I talked to my new friend Jeffrey from Milwaukee. Over 50 years later Jeffrey and I are still friends. His mother and my father both suffered the same unfortunate Alzheimer end.

As high school graduation marked a thankful goodbye to Shaker, I wondered whether this was a forever goodbye to Betsy who had one more year at Shaker until she would have to choose a college. Would we survive apart?

Before I left we had one glorious summer as counselors at adjacent camps without supervision and with my new Volkswagen to take us to private hideaways on off days. It would be hard to say goodbye.

"OH RICHIE, you say the funniest things!"
says Betsy Geller at the Hi-Y Fall Ball.

32

CHAPTER 3: WISCONSIN 1962

OVER 50 YEARS AGO I became a freshman at the University of Wisconsin. In 1962, JFK had been our president for two years. The Bay of Pigs had already happened. Marilyn Monroe had been found dead in her bedroom. Ken Kesey published "Cuckoo's Nest" and James Meredith registered at Ole Miss. A new guy Bob Dylan was being talked about by the hip kids from New York. The "times were a changing." I was hoping they would change for me as well.

There were only a few of us going to Wisconsin from Shaker so I would not carry the metaphoric "old baggage." I would not be Betsy's boyfriend, the "dancing guy" or the guy who apparently was not smart enough to be asked to take any Advanced Placement Classes. I was the guy who felt an enormous responsibility to excel at college and be the one person in the family who would earn a degree. This was not to be a vacation.

My parents waved goodbye in Cleveland and I flew United to Chicago, traveling light with only a couple of bags, and then took North Central Airlines to Madison. The North Central flight was a chewing gum plane that didn't sit parallel to the ground. You angled up to your seat where you could light up a cigarette if you wanted and chewed gum to keep from losing your lunch while the plane bounced around at low altitude.

I was enrolled in Adams Hall, one of the school dormitories on the north side of the hill, reasonably far away from the private dorms and the fraternities which were all on the south side of the hill. I was in one of the "farmer" dorms, called that because most of these dorms on the north side were populated with Wisconsin kids right off the farm.

33

From 1840 to 1880, Wisconsin was considered "America's breadbasket" because one-sixth of the wheat grown in the nation came from Wisconsin. But wheat was hard on the soil. As yields fell so did prices and farmer's started to look elsewhere to "feed crops." Dairy farming took over, helped by technology and training at the University of Wisconsin and the German and Scandinavian immigrant families who specialized in the European-style cheeses. Wisconsin became known for its Swiss cheese and became the leading dairy state in the nation, producing more butter and cheese than any other state.

One of my first friends, Terry, was living on a local farm before school. He was a sweet kid who wanted to study to be a meteorologist and be a weatherman on TV. Several weeks after school started Terry found out I was Jewish. He asked if he could feel my head. I asked why. He said he had heard that Jews had horns. He was not being intentionally offensive, he was just curious.

My roommate who would share my tiny room was not off the farm but rather off the planet. He was a "pocket protector," slide rule kid with the top shirt button buttoned. He had a robotic like sound and cadence to his voice a preview of what I would hear form a famous astrophysicist. In all fairness he treated me as well as I deserved since I avoided him as often as possible. Today, I cannot even remember his name.

But as I became comfortable exploring the campus, it was clear I was living on the wrong side of town and would not meet kids that had a background similar to mine. The Jews were on the other side of the hill. And they were not like any Jewish kids I had ever met before. The fraternities were already having their early rush so, out of curiosity, I checked it out. My dad in his day was the president of his ZBT fraternity at Ohio State and so I was a "legacy," someone they had an informal obligation to accept. The truth was I wanted nothing to do with a fraternity. The last thing I wanted was a new label. But I was invited to some parties and so I went. It was the "Animal House" era.

The kids were mostly from two tribes, neither one of which resembled my own. There were the rich Highland Park Jews and the cool New Yorkers. Chicago kids all wore the same uniform: Bass Weejun loafers, khaki pants and yellow or blue Gant shirts. The New York kids wore early Army surplus. The New Yorkers to my astonishment read the paper every day, visited the student union for collective conversation about current events, and knew what was going on, not just in sports but in the world. If either group was asked about my tribe they would have used the label: "goyim Jews" or possibly "poor midwestern secular."

Once classes started I spent little time at Adams Hall. I had free time and spent most of it at the library. I took a written test and a physical test that allowed me to "pass" on gym. An essay I wrote, after it was reviewed, allowed me to pass on freshman English. I had a lot of time to explore the campus and Madison.

I was chasing a Bachelor in Science instead of a Bachelor in Arts so I could avoid any foreign language requirement. But I was feeling guilty about the cost of college without a vocation in mind and felt that I should actually learn how to do something, so I also enrolled in the commerce school. It required one semester of a basic accounting course. A little more about that later.

But suddenly, overnight, school stopped. Was school over? Was everything over?

Someone turned out the lights. Everyone I knew left school and went home to possibly die with their families. I could not afford the long trip home, even by greyhound, so I remained at school during what we later learned was called the Cuban Missile Crisis. It lasted from October 22-28. When it was over, I remember thinking it was time to start reading the paper. I didn't want to die ignorant of basic current events. Having survived, I became more confident that the world would not end while I was at school. But if I was going to love college I needed to try to find somewhere else to live. The problem was that my parents had signed a mandatory one-year contract at Adams Hall. Somehow I needed to break the contract.

I found the manager of the dorm (also a midwestern Jew) and did my best to describe how unhappy and suicidal I felt in the dorm.

"Could I please just move out?"

His response was to suggest I get immediate mental health counseling. Not liking his response, I suggested we cut the shit.

"What do I have to do to get out of here."

His response was: "There is nothing you can do."

A brain storm hit, and I said:

"I forgot to put on the application that I eat only kosher food. I can't eat at the dorm cafeteria." I was sure this would work.

But he responded: "Not a problem, we can make an accommodation for you. You are not the only kid that has ever requested kosher food."

Now pissed, I responded, "Maybe, but I am the only kid who is going to show up every day dressed like a Sephardic Jew. I am also going to, with great gusto and volume, shout the prayers over bread at each meal."

To make sure he understood I began shouting: "Baruch atah adonai eloheinu melech ha'olam."

I think he admired my attempt or believed I was crazy because he compromised by allowing me to move out at the end of the semester with no penalty. And I did. Into the ZBT house, before I had even pledged.

I am not sure why they let me move in without being a "brother" but maybe it was because they didn't have anyone in the fraternity exactly like me and after all I was a legacy, or maybe because they found me an interesting amusement. And they didn't have anyone in the house who didn't dress like them. I hardly had any clothes and what I had I wore every day. My outfit, was a maroon sweater and a green corduroy sport coat with brown patches on the elbows. I had chugga boots with two eyelets. No hat or gloves.

The rent they wanted to charge me was less than what I was paying at the dorm but I would have to figure out food. I couldn't eat at the house without being a brother.

So I got a meal job.

My first meal job was at the one Jewish fraternity you pledged if you were certain you would never get into any of the others. The so-called "loser" fraternity. I was the new employee so I didn't get to wait on tables. I was Mr. Pots and Pans. This was actually a good gig because I didn't have to be there while the meal was being served. I could come in anytime, just so I got the work done.

The cook, Essee, approved of my efforts and let me eat whatever I wanted from the current day's meal or the one before. She had the weird belief that if she put a drop of iodine on her tongue every day she would never get sick. If I doubted my memory, 45 years later on an OAT trip to Viet Nam, I met someone who had the same job a few years later with Essee. She was still using the iodine.

So now I was set with a place to live and meals but I needed a little spending money. My parents and grandfather paid the tuition but that was it. I was on my own for the rest unless I became desperate and needed help. I never did. I worked in a ladies shoe store for a few months until they suggested I buy some clothes if I wanted to remain working there. My next job was cleaning a kitchen at a real restaurant.

Meanwhile I was studying hard and enjoying my freedom. For the first time in many months, I was self-absorbed and not thinking about Larry my parents or Betsy. The difficulty communicating with Ohio in some ways made it easier to become a true Wisconsinite. I became involved with Wisconsin's Symposium and remember George Wallace coming to speak while I was an usher. My first taste of politics.

Freshman classes usually involved a large lecture where you did not interact with the professor. Later in the week you would meet with the quiz instructor who usually was a graduate student. If you actually attended the lectures (most of my friends did not) and met the quiz instructor, a grad student just a few years old than you, you probably got a much better grade. I knew all my quiz instructors and also frequently had coffee with them at the student union. These relationships had their ups and downs.

I found the courses interesting and after Shaker frankly easy. But maybe it was just because I was studying harder. My advanced algebra course was easier than the algebra course I had taken at Shaker. I had a perfect score on all the tests at the time my quiz instructor and student union friend invited me to join a club he thought I might enjoy. He described it as a club where a lot of New York kids discussed current events. I signed up but for some reason, I can no longer recall, never actually went to a single meeting. My failure to attend proved persuasive when many years later my brief inadvertent membership in the SDS (Students for a Democratic Society) was causing concern with my ethics approval required to take the Attorney Bar in Ohio. Somehow I was on the FBI radar screen and my membership had to be explained before I could become an attorney.

I also had become friends with my accounting professor and told her I made a mistake becoming part of the Commerce School and wanted to drop accounting, which was eating up too much of my time with its time consuming homework. I had an A going at the time we discussed my wanting to drop the course. She told me to be careful that to drop a course you had to do it in the first six weeks. Apparently I forgot that and in week seven went to my dean and asked to drop the course. He said: "You are too late." There was no discussion. The fact that I was doing well was irrelevant. He told me that if I had had a better excuse relating to sickness or a family problem he might have considered my request, but not liking the Commerce track was not good enough.

I stormed out of his office mad as hell and never went back to accounting. The quiz instructor who liked me gave me a C for the semester as a gift for being her friend. I would pay more attention to the rules in the future.

One of those rules related to social courtesy. My unacceptable conduct sent me back to the dean's office.

I was not dating at all in college. I can't explain why except that Betsy was on my mind and I felt dating would be unfair to her. I suspected she was dating but some sense of honor made it taboo for me. My ZBT roommate asked me to take out his girlfriend's roommate as a favor to his girlfriend. He said she was actually beautiful and was in fact in a Wrigley's chewing gum commercial on television. He offered his car for the evening.

The early part of the date went fairly well. She really was beautiful and we had a fairly normal initial conversation. But she didn't like the first restaurant I suggested and wanted to talk about nothing but her commercial, as if she had won the academy award. Her exaggerated feelings of self-importance finally drove me a bit mad and I pulled the car to the curb a few blocks from the student union and told her to get out.

She said: "You're kidding?"

I said: "I am not. Get out!"

She said: "You can't be serious".

I said: "I am."

She finally did get out and reported me to the Dean. This was serious and but for my excellent grades could have been fatal. I was put on social probation. I wasn't sure what that meant but I guess it was like strike one, maybe two.

It was not until my third year of college that I began to realize that I was not as stupid as Latin and Shaker had made me feel. I had almost all A's except for Accounting and Geography. I figured Geography would be an easy science but it turned out to be extremely challenging. You learned about tectonics and isobars and all the natural sciences. No high school geography maps were involved. It was tough but fascinating. But what really turned the corner for me was when my first full professor called on me and addressed me as Mr. Schwachter and seemed genuinely interested in what I had to say.

When it became time to join ZBT or move out of the house I elected to stay and became a pledge. I managed to avoid most of the pledge nonsense by saying I had to go to work. It was generally accepted that I was the one ZBT who was without deep pockets or in my case any pockets whatsoever. Also no member wanted to mess with the guy who was writing their history and English papers for a small fee. (Anything less than a B and they got their money back).

But when the final "hell week" started, I had lost patience with the whole silly nonsense and was ready to quit. The final night event was staged to keep us up all night blindfolded in our room with African music blasting (Babatunde Olatunji). We were then taken to the "sacred room" where we would become members or wash out. The trick was to tell us separately that we didn't make it. And wait for us to cry or get hysterical and then they would say: "Just kidding you made it". This routine was probably older than my grandfather's Rotary Club.

I actually did not know the script but when they told me I didn't make it I just replied:

"Fine, I was only becoming a member because I didn't want to look for a new place."

My sponsor told me to please not tell the brothers what I said. I did not and respected his love of something I found silly.

40

In my third year, Betsy had finally come to visit. She went to a frat event with me and of course all the fraternity brothers fell in love with her and suggested once again "what the hell was she doing with me, much less sleeping with me in the Lorraine Hotel." To sleep in the hotel with Betsy required a diversion to get around the guard who protected all the young supposedly virginal visitors. I'm not sure how we did it but it did involve walking up at least six flights of stairs to sneak to her room.

My final year of Wisconsin was fantastic. The truth was that I had already earned enough credits to graduate by the end of my third year and so didn't even need to go back to Madison for the fourth. This time I returned to Madison with money I had saved during the summer at Camp Roosevelt and with a course selection that was one hundred percent fun. Basically I took one art history course and every English course I had always dreamed of taking if I didn't need a political science degree and a B.S. This new curriculum allowed me to lie in bed all day and read.

Betsy had tried out a college career at Michigan State but apparently was not that enthusiastic. She returned to Cleveland and was working in a retail store. We were still an item and in fact I had taken the Greyhound home more often to see her.

Roe v. Wade was not the law of the land in 1965. Abortion was not legal, but like prostitution, the law did not stop nature's calling and particularly unwanted pregnancies. Every spring break and after Christmas break, girls would come back to Madison and get admitted to the hospital because they had received a botched illegal procedure in Chicago.

Today you can go to the drug store and know in minutes whether you are pregnant. In '65 you had to go to the doctor as Mr. and Mrs. and see whether you killed the rabbit or not. The test could take some time, during which you drank too much and slept too little.

41

Betsy and I went through this nightmare. How it was resolved is not part of this narrative. But it certainly brought us closer together. Close enough for me to ask Betsy's father if he would approve my getting engaged to his daughter. He seemed relieved to say yes. Dr. Jac and I had become buddies.

Aside from my English and art courses, I decided to take an advertising course. I was a fan of the periodical Advertising Age and was always interested in ad copy and ad presentation. A few weeks into the course our professor gave us an assignment to enter the Hershey chocolate contest. Hershey had never advertised in print media, apparently never feeling it was necessary. Now they were going to advertise in print for the first time and the contest was to create a campaign.

My approach was to riff on the successful Volkswagen ads which had spartan copy and a large picture of a Beetle. My campaign featured a solo picture of a large Hershey bar, an American flag and the slogan: "Hershey, the Great American Chocolate Bar". I have heard that slogan since and wondered. My layout and copy won a regional award and I was off and dreaming of applying to the Northwestern School of Journalism, which offered advertising courses.

But that wouldn't happen because I was engaged and already accepted at Case Western Reserve Law School in Cleveland. The school was happy to have me without requiring me to take the new law school admission test.

My fate was sealed. But before my return to Cleveland there would be a little more excitement. One night I took a break from my new meal job at a girl's private dorm and went to the fraternity house for a dinner. They were electing officers for the fraternity. There were speeches and arguments and then as a joke someone put me up for an office. I declined to speak but in some kind of a protest vote I was elected treasurer, which was a good thing because that office allowed me to go to the national convention in San Francisco the following month on the frat's dollar. The house bought my ticket direct from

Chicago on a jet. I turned in the ticket for a prop flight and droned on but pocketed the savings for spending money in San Francisco.

Something else changed my life that year. Humorology was a fraternity-sorority event that was the hottest ticket every year. The fraternities and sororities would pair off to create a Broadway style original mini musical to be performed before the entire Wisconsin audience. Original songs, and original story and choreography. Awards like Tony's were given out for the best in several categories.

The Humorology committee produced the show. To be on the committee was political because the it also decided the fraternity sorority groupings for the event. I was drafted to be on the committee probably because I was known as an outsider, not a real frat fan, and not from Chicago or New York. The thought was that I would be objective and not favor ZBT, often a winner no matter who they were paired with.

Katherine was also on the committee. I had never seen her before. It's hard not to be drawn to someone who seems strangely and obviously interested in you. It took one date before we became a couple and I was sure I was falling in love. In a few dates she knew most of what there was to know about me, including Betsy.

I learned later that her father was superintendent of schools in a Chicago suburb and that Katherine was a super athlete and scholar. But she was also irreverent, sneaking out of her sorority house at night to be with me, going on extended trips to Chicago with me. Weekends at Wisconsin Dells. What was I thinking? I was engaged to Betsy! What I should have been thinking is what Katherine already knew,: I was not ready to be married. I was not ready to go to law school. I was not ready to move back to Cleveland.

Betsy was invited and was coming to Humorology. Katherine and I were giving an award together. She sat next to Betsy during the ceremony. Betsy returned to Cleveland. If she suspected my affair she said nothing. None of my friends ratted me out. In a few weeks I would go home to marry. Katherine was amused by my dilemma but never pushed me to alter my course. She knew I was also not ready for Betsy or Katherine. There was no way I could perform my codependent ritual with Katherine. I think she loved me but she clearly didn't need me.

CHAPTER 4: CLEVELAND 1969

I AM NOT SURE what my life would have been like if I had not moved back to Cleveland. I am sure Katherine and I would not have stayed together. She would have eventually dumped me. I was too serious for her. Would I have gone on to Northwestern? Worked on Madison Avenue for an ad agency or possibly a small town newspaper? Found Lois Lane? In the quantum world maybe all those alternatives have occurred beyond my consciousness.

What I do know happened is that we had a backyard wedding the following summer at Betsy's house complete with a few of our friends and many, many of Betsy's and my parents' friends. The actual ceremony was performed in her living room with 100 seated guests to hear me say:

"Harei at m'kudeshet li b'tabaat zo k'dat Moshe v'Yisrael".

"Behold, you are consecrated for/ to me, with this ring, according to the religion/ tradition of Moses and Israel.

I would love to have had 10% of the money spent on the extravagance of that reality show. And then off we went to Bermuda for a honeymoon complete with an airline strike that added time to the event. One more pause before reality. There was hardly time to think. The wedding and then the immediate start of law school.

What motivates high school sweethearts to marry? They knew early on they had met their better half? They knew that their life would not be complete without the person they met in high school. They just happily accepted that marriage was the next level in their forever relationship? They were linked in a codependent relationship?

I loved Betsy then as I do now. But I wanted to be my own better half. I didn't want anyone to complete me, to make me whole. I knew I had to do that myself. I had to be my own rock. And then there was that codependency thing that I knew I could fall back into. I feared

46

reoccupying that role. So the happy couple moved into their first apartment, a new kind of dorm but this time as coed newlyweds. One car transported the law student to school and his wife to downtown Cleveland and the bank where she worked as a teller.

If there was another person in my law school class who was married I never met him. Lots of students were out partying and bar hopping. Lots playing softball on the law school team. None that I knew going home to their Mrs. I had no idea what to expect from law school. The only lawyer I knew was a friend of my father and he was my father's boss. I wasn't even sure what lawyers did who weren't fighting for civil rights or keeping people from going to jail.

In 1966 Case Western Law was not the "A" law school it is now. It did have interesting, bright students and young, engaging teachers. Most of the new teachers were from Harvard, recruited by the new dean. The majority of the students were local from Ohio colleges. I realized quickly that if I was to become a lawyer, whatever that meant, I would have to work hard at school. To my surprise law school was well suited for how my brain worked. Memorization, essential for medical school, was useless in law school. You would never find a legal case that exactly fit the fact pattern of your new situation. You had to think and you had to reason from older situations to your new situation. Being clever was more rewarded than being smart. Whatever smart means. High IQ was not enough.

Most of what you learn in law school that is important you learn in the first year. How to think like a lawyer and how to use the library are most of it. My grades were good, I made law review and then decided I could miss a lot of classes and be a substitute teacher in the Cleveland inner city schools and make some money.

All you needed was a college degree and you could get a temporary teaching certificate and wait for the early morning call that they needed you. It helped if you were combat ready. Middle school or junior high was dangerous. The kids weren't old enough to realize that there were consequences to outrageous behavior. Each morning you were issued a paddle and told to respond accordingly to aberrant behavior. Fearing for my dignity, if not my life, I stopped substitute teaching at the junior high schools and hoped to get called for the high schools where kids, particularly 12th graders, were close enough to their high school diploma to want to keep from being expelled.

I always ignored the teacher's curriculum for the week and taught black history, which seemed to interest my temporary students and has always interested me. I kept away from the law, except constitutional law as it applied to civil rights, since these kids knew more about criminal law than I. Their families had a lot of hands on experience. I remember the spelling test I was supposed to administer and grade. I asked the kids if they knew the meaning of all the words on the list. Many did not.

The summer after my second year of law school I was a summer intern at one of the best Jewish law firms. This internship was normally a guarantee that you would be hired after graduation. When I graduated the economy was brutal and they hired no one. The summer experience was not that interesting and should have convinced me to give up the law, but I needed a job and a career and I was married. I saw no other alternative but to forge onward.

In April of my last year of school, shortly before graduation, my first son Steven David was born. I had not yet graduated, I had not yet passed the Bar which wouldn't be offered until July, and I had not yet nailed down a job. And Lyndon still wanted me for Viet Nam. Just a little pressure. Steven also didn't come with an instruction manual. I did hit four home runs at four at bats at the law school picnic, which was a bit of redemption for the guy who kept making excuses not to play on the law school softball team.

The draft thing got resolved when I managed to get classified as medically unfit for duty. My brother had been 4F so I guess it was a sibling thing to flunk out. I had assembled medical reports from my allergist, who confirmed that I was allergic to everything on earth. These were not persuasive. The medical officer asked if those were my real glasses. I said of course. He said: "What the fuck are you worried about?" It turned out if you had a refractive error worse than minus eight in one eye you were not going to cut it. I was worse in both eyes. I always had coke bottle lenses until contacts and finally cataract surgery, which restored my vision to 20/20.

Shortly thereafter I became employed courtesy of Lady Bird Johnson. The managing partner of the law firm that ultimately employed me owned radio stations. He was more entrepreneur than attorney. His newest project was to expand his media holdings by purchasing an outdoor billboard business. He mentioned this to me in my first interview, basically making conversation while eating easily a two pound bag of cashews. The company he was considering purchasing competed with the giant in the industry. In order to complete his due diligence he needed to know the locations of his competitor's sites. And he needed it quickly.

I had an idea. I asked him, between his mouthfuls of nuts, if I got that information for him would that raise his interest in my employment prospects. He just smiled.

Two days later I had a meeting at the competitor's office. The manager of the local office was very anxious to see me. I had told him on the phone that I was a law student writing a law review article on Lady Bird's proposed Highway Beautification Act and wanted his comments on the proposed law. Of course the law horrified him and would play havoc with some of his installations. I asked him to give me the exact data on the impact. He did. As expected, the report included a print out of each of the competitor's sites.

Deceitful? Yes. But it got me employed at the law firm. My boss was very impressed. I started work shortly after I took the bar exam with expected results from the test not due until months later. If I flunked I expected to be fired.

The bar exam was held in Columbus, Ohio, a few hour drive from Cleveland. Back then the exam was all essay and lasted three days with a morning and afternoon session. Everyone I knew went a few days early and made themselves crazy studying the last hours in the same local hotel, walking distance to the exam. I did not want to do that.

Instead I stayed at a married friend's apartment in Columbus. He was an intern at a hospital there and I had known him since nursery school. We had a nice dinner the night before the exam and I was relaxed and happy to be in the apartment away from the crazy nervous schoolmates. The morning of the exam his wife was to take me while my friend slept from his all night work at the hospital. As we were leaving their cat shot out the door. We were <u>not</u> going to the exam until the cat was captured and returned. I finally arrived at the exam a wreck minutes before it started.

Flair pens had just become popular and as a lefty who printed I loved them. Since I arrived late, I missed the early do's and don'ts of the exam preliminaries, where it was explained that you were not to use flair pens. They were not a proven writing instrument and the concern was that the ink would not dry properly and the exam book would become impossible to read.

Another option was to type your answers in a special typing room. There was a legendary story, probably not true, about someone who was typing his answers when his ribbon no longer printed. Instead of finishing with a pen, the test taker just sat there in shock.

I completed the three days of essays and knew in my heart that I had done really well. I knew what to say and how to say it. I love essay exams because you can always imply you know more than you actually do. I left very confident. As I was walking out the door the final day I learned for the first time about the flair pen ban. From July until October when the results were announced I had nightmares of an ink schmeared answer book. Thankfully I passed and in fact had placed in the top five in the state. Maybe neatness and the flare pen actually helped. My printing is very easy to read.

My new job was located in the Terminal Tower, Cleveland's only skyscraper. Cleveland in the 70's was not a happy place. By one account Cleveland had lost over 20% of its population. It had defaulted on its bonds and had become a mob town sometimes called Bomb City USA. The Cuyahoga river was dead and Lake Erie was dying as was the steel industry. Randy Newman described it sarcastically in a song he titled "Burn On:"

Cleveland, city of light, city of magic
Cleveland, city of light, you're calling me
Cleveland, even now I can remember
'Cause the Cuyahoga River
Goes smokin' through my dreams

Burn on, big river, burn on
Burn on, big river, burn on
Now the Lord can make you tumble
And the Lord can make you turn
And the Lord can make you overflow
But the Lord can't make you burn

I carried my new briefcase to work each day and wore my new suit and button down shirt with rep tie. I resisted the popular wingtip shoes. My early sign of rebellion. I wore the uniform reluctantly while the rest of the young people I knew, not yet married or even employed were wearing tie dye shirts and smoking weed.

I watched newsreels of the Woodstock festival that had attracted over 400,000 people guessing they were copulating in the rain while I was brief writing. Apparently there was a new understanding of what was important, an indoctrination into a new lifestyle while I was being indoctrinated into the old. The one where law firms were split along religious lines, private eating clubs excluded women, and the country club you belonged to played an important part in your future success, as did your golfing prowess.

The lack of modern technology made the pace of things in a law firm much slower than they are today. All documents were typed on a typewriter with several carbon copies. It was still pre affordable Xerox. Errors were fixed with "white out." Word processing machines were not yet invented at least for office use. The entire top floor of the Mellon Bank in Pittsburgh was a room full of giant IBM computers cooled with massive fans that together accomplished less than the current phone in my pocket. We did research in the library and disappeared for hours hunting down the right cases in a Shepardizing effort that would now take minutes on the computer.

I worked directly for one of the partners who was famous for not wanting any help and burning through first year associates. For reasons that probably had more to do with my relationship with some of the most attractive secretaries in downtown Cleveland than my abilities, he became comfortable with me. He actually liked me. And in a familiar pattern for me unloaded his personal issues to me and expected me to share my own. We fed off each other like good codependents do. I fixed his occasional mess and he promoted me, but not to the extent that he might lose me to another firm.

I was very good in court for surprising reasons. Most judges were not the brightest lights, and even if they were they were lazy. If you did their work for them you almost always won. This involved writing "findings of fact" and "conclusions of law" concisely in a manner that spelled out clearly why your client must win. If done well these "findings of fact" and "conclusions of law" more often than not would become the exact ruling of the judge.

After a year or two of wins I became confident enough to not be intimidated by some of the more prominent attorneys in town. One notable example occurred in a divorce case I was handling. It had as opposing counsel, a highly regarded but feared nasty New York Jew who loved to intimidate young lawyers. He requested a conference at his firm, attorney to attorney. When I got to his office his secretary told me to go in and I found him on his back on the couch half asleep

52

with his pants undone for belly relief. He looked up but didn't get up and just said he wasn't in the mood anymore for our meeting.

"Come back some other day or better yet never."

I looked him right in the eye and told him "Go fuck yourself."

He immediately jumped up and I thought he was going to try and hit me or at least his pants would fall down. Instead he hugged me, loved my response ("You've got balls") and asked me if I wanted to leave that ass you work for and join him.

"Boychik, I've heard good things."

I was doing well in court but was probably disappointing my boss who expected I'd bring in more business. He wanted my father-in-law's, the great Dr. Geller's, friends as clients. That wasn't going to happen. They would have to keep me for my skill not my connections. I was already beginning to resent them. I learned quickly that connections counted more than skills in the 70's in Cleveland and ultimately it's why I quit.

One of our clients operated landfills in several of the Cleveland suburbs. and every year they held a massive all day party at the opening day of the baseball season. Every judge and respected lawyer was invited, as well as every hooker in the city. The company's newest landfill bucked up against the zoning laws. The affected suburban city always did their best to stop construction. I argued that the zoning laws didn't cover a landfill because it actually was not a use of the land covered by zoning; we just dug a hole and then filled it up. When we were done you could finally use the land and only then would the zoning laws come to play. My novel argument won.

Later at the baseball party the big boss came over to congratulate me but said:

"Don't get too cocky, it was fixed."

I had, however, other moments that did made me proud to be a lawyer. I argued a case before the US Court of Appeals in Cincinnati. On the three judge panel was Anthony Joseph Celebrezze, Sr. who served as the 49th mayor of Cleveland and as a cabinet member in the Kennedy and Johnson administrations. I won that case and months later Celebrezze came over to our firm's lunch table in a restaurant we often frequented for weekly meetings. My boss was excited to have him acknowledge our firm with a hello. He shook some hands and then unexpectedly patted my shoulder and said:

"This young man did a fabulous job in my court. You found yourself a great young lawyer. We all should expect great things from him in the future."

Be still my heart.

Meanwhile back at the home front. We had moved from our initial law school apartment to a townhouse in another part of town and finally to our first home one block from the house I was born in. Betsy was a new realtor and successfully figured a way for us to buy our "starter home."

My youngest son was born just 18 months after Steven. Betsy had her hands full. I was gone every day and usually came home to controlled chaos. But things were good and although I was chasing the secretaries around downtown Cleveland and telling my share of lies about my activities, I was keeping my pants on. But that was becoming an effort. In my mind everyone was getting laid except me.

My boss and I were rewarded with a trip to New York for winning an important case. We went to dinner in a restaurant that involved navigating escargot. If you watched Julia Roberts in Pretty Woman you get the picture. I had no idea what to do with those little snails in the shell.

After dinner my boss took me to an apartment where I soon discovered two "ladies of the evening" ready to perform their prearranged duties. I could see my boss on his back through a half open door getting fellatio from a young pro. I told my "lady" that I was happily married and hoped she would allow me to just fake it. "Please play along." No problem for her. Afterwards my boss was eager to know how it went for me.

"Did you come?"

"Because if you didn't we're going back right now."

I wasn't sure what the correct answer was.

Meanwhile, since it looked like my career was moving along smoothly and Betsy and I seemed to be settled with our completed family and elite country club status, Betsy said we should buy a new house in Shaker. I believe now, reminiscent of my earlier disastrous move to Shaker to start junior high school, that the purchase of the new house was the beginning of our marriage derailment.

The new house was bigger but to my eye a disjointed mess. It was on a main thoroughfare that separated University Height from Shaker Heights. The kids would go to one of the best elementary schools. The front yard was mostly dirt with virtually no landscaping. It was a good price but needed lots of work. I did not want to move but felt Betsy deserved this. She had the bulk of the stay at home work and the house had a bigger kitchen and a family room and lots to keep her busy in the future fixing it up. I reminded her that it was a "fixer upper" and it wouldn't happen overnight. But frankly money was her department. I didn't need any because I was never anywhere where I had a chance to spend. I was at home or at work.

I actually spent the summer painting the house myself with one ladder. A crazy stunt. The rabbi who liked to walk to temple on the Sabbath loved to stop by on his journey to watch me go at it. I also dug up the front yard and planted new grass. But the inside was still a mess. Unexpectedly Betsy announced that her parents had decided to pay for us to fix up the inside. We purchased new carpeting, some furniture and hired some major kitchen remodeling. We bought some furniture from the May Company at a dramatic discount based on Betsy's grandfather's prior status as an original member of the Board.

Could this gift be true? Actually it was not.

I was getting bored at the law firm and tired of the rapid transit ride to the Terminal Tower. As an occasional reward to myself I would drive down and enjoy the radio in transit and try to become familiar with the popular music now featured on Cleveland's new FM radio. I still didn't get it and discovered an early version of NPR which played mostly classical music. I did not like the Beatles or the Stones. I was a Miles Davis man.

If you drove to work you parked in the garage under the terminal tower. The parking fee for the day was two dollars, which at the time was excessive on a 10K a year salary. When you left the lot at the end of the day you would hand your ticket to the ticket guy and every day he would announce the same thing.

"It's just two dollars."

It was the "just" part that infuriated me. It was "just" to maybe a few of the people who parked here, but not to me. Every time I parked there it ate at me a little more until I finally said to myself if he says that one more time I'm never parking here again, and in fact, screw this job I'm never coming here again. He said it, and shortly thereafter I quit my job.

The firm tried to keep me from leaving by offering a little more money and appealing to my ego. Another firm also tried to recruit me, but I was interested in a complete change that didn't involve downtown Cleveland. One of the partners in my current firm was a Doan Electric son and my hero. Herb's family owned Doan, the largest electrical contracting company in the Midwest. Every time Adolph, Herb's father and President of Doan, got angry with someone he would ask me to sue, so I knew him well. Herb was too busy having fun to deal with his father. He respected my legal ability and knew Adolph would be a great reference for me. Herb said that someone he knew well, a very successful real estate developer was looking for in house counsel. Was I interested? You bet.

I met Sidney Simon President of American Housing Systems, and was hired to become his in house counsel. I learned quickly that what an in house counsel actually did was reduce the costs of the outside law firm. Simon still relied on the big firm but now could argue that they should cut their fees since "if you don't Richard will do it." I was glad they were handling most of the work since I really was not qualified.

What Sydney needed was a new friend, and for that task I excelled. The boy who loved dependent relationships. If you saw Sophie's Choice you heard a version of Sydney's nightmare. I learned his story on one of our business trips. Sophie's choice was to give up her son or daughter to the Germans on the way to the death camps. Sidney didn't make a choice but his act of kindness got his brother killed.

Sidney's entire family was in a concentration camp. When his brother fell ill and had the chills, Sydney gave his brother his coat to wear. Apparently because of the coat his brother was wearing he was picked for the gas chamber before Sydney, who managed to last until he was liberated. Being a "guilt survivor" loomed large in his behavior when I worked there. It was evident in his gambling trips to Vegas, where he usually lost, and his very risky business decisions. I learned a lot from Sydney and worked on an early syndication deal in Kissimmee, Florida when Disney first began its new venture there.

I heard Herb was leaving the firm, and he asked me if I wanted to join up with him in a new financial enterprise. I didn't need details. It was Herb. I said yes and said goodbye to Sydney on good terms.

Eden Financial lasted three years, during which time I developed a strong personal friendship with Herb but learned I was better off on my own. Herb was supposed to be the safety net with his family's scraps for us to work on. The only "bread and butter" work was the eviction business. Herb's family owned some high rise apartment buildings in East Cleveland that housed a lot of minority residents on the edge of poverty and a lot who were not but who were engaged in less than legal enterprises. I was a large percentage of the municipal courts docket. But I was good to the tenants that were being evicted and did not put people on the street where their property would be quickly stolen by their former neighbors. The judge figured our party room was his to use as he chose and he'd throw his parties there and never clean up. That was better than charging for each eviction.

We also arranged a few syndicated deals that allowed us to purchase three shopping centers with investors. We would have done more but Herb spent most of his time with his office door shut and screaming at other members of his family. I loved Herb and he respected me, but I knew it was time to leave. I could do what we had been doing on my own. I respect the fact that Herb was not angry and wished me well.

So I was now unemployed. I was unattached from the working world. Why not complete the cycle and say goodbye to Betsy.

CHAPTER 5: EPIPHANY/IRIE

HE LEARNED THAT IF YOU HELD YOUR THUMB PARALLEL to the horizon and counted the number of stacked thumbs it took to the falling sun, times twenty minutes, that was exactly how long he had until sunset. This was useful, on the beach of Negril, Jamaica if you needed to walk eight miles to the Rock House for cocktails before it was dark. Not Cleveland, Ohio dark where there were street lights and neon signs to mark your path, but Jamaican Negril dark where only the stars and whispers from shadowed faces were there to guide you. He points to a sky so graphically exact that it could be an observatory: "Delonn, isn't that the constellation Orion?" The young Jamaican with the body of a Greek god responds:

"Sir Richard, in Jamaica we call that a bunch of stars."

****

All the government of Jamaica required was his birth certificate and $20. He hoped he packed enough clothes and that he had the proper look for the yacht club. He grew up a country club boy. Surviving the minimal customs in Montego Bay, Richard exited the airport to a field of mules and dogs. Among the many cab driver solicitations he chose the driver standing next to the '54 Buick Roadmaster that reminded him of the family car as a boy.

"Irie then, Master Richard," shouts his new driver friend Rashard.

"Welcome to Jamaica and the beautiful drive to Negril. Is this your first time?"

"It is, Rashard."

"Do you know the yacht club in Negril?"

"Yah, Man".

"Are there many boats there?"

Rashard lights a joint that would have made Cheech and Chong gag.

"No boats man". What your friend tell you?"

*****

The Northcoast Highway from Montego Bay to Negril travels around the coast for 50 miles and takes even the most aggressive cabbie two hours. Rashard got Richard to the yacht club in just under 2.5. As he dropped Richard's two large bags on a pitch dark road after sunset, Richard assumed that a golf cart or something would take him the rest of the way to the clubhouse where he would find a Dewars. Instead he saw a sign on a shack not more than twenty steps from where he stood that said by way of a twisted rope: "Yacht Club." Outside of the door stood some locals with yellow eyes who must have noticed his bewilderment and said: "You'll need a Red Stripe."

****

No electricity also means no telephone or hot water. Hot water was obtained for short periods through the pipes exposed to the sun next to the shower but that rarely lasted more than 30 seconds. To see in the dark you employed lanterns and so matches were at a premium. A Bic lighter was a gift from God. Long distance phone calls? A call to the States was an all day process. Only one hotel on the beach had an operator willing to tackle the hurdles and if you could afford it you still had to wait in the lobby most of the day to accomplish the call.

*****

Richard had been staying at Ten Sing Pinn for three days before he met Delonn, 24 hours before his epiphany. Ten Sing Pinn was run by a Brit who owned an oversized ancient gas-guzzling Jaguar that seemed totally out of place in Negril. His cottages were for those who were "short of funds." In other words, there were lots of very young people lodged in rooms about the size of Richard's stall shower.

The Brit's name was Nigel. He shared Richard's love, if not skill, at backgammon. If Richard had not been humble he could have stayed at Ten Sing for free for the rest of his life on his backgammon bounty or rather on Nigel's failure to master the doubling cube. After one particularly bloody backgammon massacre, Nigel offered Richard some magic mushrooms as payment. "You know they grow

61

right on top of shit. Very powerful." The non-pot-smoking Richard decided to try something new.

Why someone dares to drive with their hands off the steering wheel is a mystery. Richard never lost control. Ever. Until that night. Timothy Leary's arguments not withstanding, this was not a good experience for Richard. It is one thing to see the world warped into bizarre distortions in the USA and quite another in Jamaica where it's often difficult to not float into an altered consciousness merely from the presence of a less filtered nature. Stumbling down the road, commencing with the first person remarking to him; "Good mushrooms, eh?" he knew he was in trouble. As he became more and more uncomfortable in his skin, he thought that food might help. But Negril was shut down for food and actually even the bars were closed. In a full panic, he looked for help, a friendly face, an American he knew.

Suddenly finding someone he knew became the most important thing in his life. After what seemed like hours to him, he recognized no one. He felt more alone than ever before in his life. Exhausted, with no idea where he was he sat on the side of the road and laughed hysterically and then finally collapsed into a heap. He awoke with the sun to the bug-eyed stare of a very young girl.

"You alright, Richard?"

"Uh, huh. How do you know my name?"

"All the kids know Richard"

"But why?" he asks.

"You the white Rasta man. All that blond curly hair. The only USA guy who play with us. Let me get my dad to help you. He's just inside. You know my daddy Delonn?"

His epiphany was that he could survive and maybe even thrive just by being himself. Just being Richard unaided by drugs or super powers was enough to warrant an audience with the world. Everything would be IRIE.

CHAPTER 6: EARLY 80'S

BEFORE I COULD HAVE a Jamaican epiphany, I had to resolve my relationship with Betsy and figure out how to make a living on my own. After a few years in the Shaker house and squabbles over money and some deception by both parties, it was clear that the details of our disputes were less relevant than the conclusion that our relationship needed to change. With hindsight I believe the word "divorce" was too harsh. We needed to become two independent separate entities that shared only one goal now: raising two kids. Later she might have said it was because I was screwing my secretary, and I might have said it was because she fell in love with her sewing machine; but even if both of those things were true, they were just symptoms of the greater inevitability.

The mechanics of our divorce were accomplished without argument. The vocabulary was different then but essentially we had an uncontested divorce and something like shared parenting. The kids were staying with their mother but I would live only a few miles away.

One of my brother's old friends, who was also an attorney, had purchased, a large mansion with servants' quarters and a guest house. He rented both. I leased the servants' quarters and moved in almost immediately.

Since I had already been married and already had kids, my sole interest in women was simply to find some company to add to a limited social life. I thought I did not want a "live in" or anything approaching something serious.

My office was in my new home. My sole tools were a typewriter and a phone. The business transition was working better than the social one. The first recognition that my life without my children and Betsy was going to be challenging occurred on Thanksgiving. I deluded myself into thinking that I would be invited to have thanksgiving with Betsy and the kids. There was no logical reason for me to believe I would be asked to join them but I had made no other plans. I might have had other alternatives but I really didn't search them out. One of my friends and his wife invited all those similarly disposed on turkey day to stop over, but for some reason I didn't seriously consider this. It was Cleveland so the bars were open and I knew that was a possible end to my day. But what to do during the day when everyone was with family? I was never a football fan so I decided to go to a movie. Pick one, any one.

I knew nothing about Midnight Express but that is the movie I randomly picked. You know the one where an American student is caught smuggling drugs out of Turkey. Oliver Stone's total downer. I left the movie needing a drink and a hug. I got the drink but not the hug.

As the hours slipped away at our neighborhood bar it finally occurred to me that the lemon in my vodka was not turkey and that I probably was not going to have a Thanksgiving dinner. What the hell, I would go to the losers party. But when I got there it was just the three of us having another drink with a turkey carcass completely picked over. I would plan better for the holidays in the future.

When I had the kids over to my new apartment, I actually had more fun with them than I would have had at home. They had my full attention. And they were young and I had toys, early versions of computer toys. But I would have to be more careful with them than I was at my old home. One afternoon when my new landlord was out of town we went swimming in his indoor pool. Normally off limits. The kids played until I decided to dive in and fly to the other side so quickly that I smashed my fingers into the other side of the pool. My index finger was bent back at a right angle to my hand. In my panic I just grabbed it and put it back in place. No further action was taken but I became more aware that when I was alone with the kids I had more responsibility than before.

Betsy seemed to be already setting up shop with her new love interest, Jon, who eventually would become her husband and still is today. I actually knew Jon before I knew Betsy. We both suffered together as children at our respective parents' common country club, too long a drive from home with too little for us to do as children.

At this point I was just happy that Betsy had one "partner" to deal with. I had seen how too many boyfriends could be very hard on little children. I didn't date many women who had children and if I did, I certainly would not wake up in the morning in their bed without having previously been introduced to the children.

I was in the real estate syndication business. Essentially what this meant is that I formed partnerships with investors to buy income producing properties. For my efforts arranging the transaction and then managing it I earned fees and a small equity participation in the deal. Before they changed the tax laws in 1986 it was easier to get high income investors to participate.

Any sixth grader would tell you that your profit is the difference between the money you take in and the money you pay out. In a real estate investment, depreciation is an "out" that you don't pay for until you sell the property. So even if you have excess cash on the "in and out" basis, for IRS purposes you have a loss. Depreciation (not a cash expense) is still an "out."

Before 1986 if you had losses from your investment you could apply those losses to offset your ordinary income. So if you had a $100,000 loss for tax purposes, were in the combined state and federal 50% tax bracket, and invested $50,000 the investment actually cost you nothing. You would have to pay up at the end when the property was sold but then the tax rate was lower (capital gains) and hopefully the property had appreciated for a net gain.

I had become an expert on the tax and partnership laws at the time. The problem was finding properties to buy and investors to invest. I started by approaching a shopping center owner I had met years ago with Sidney and asked him if he had anything he wanted to sell. He did not but he had a broker friend who I should meet. I arrived

65

at our first meeting dressed in jeans and my cowboy boots, my new uniform now that I was my own boss. The broker asked:

"Should we wait until your dad shows up?"

When I told him I talked to me on the phone not my dad. That my father lived in Florida and was retired. He seemed disappointed. He did have a great strip center for sale that was my ideal model for purchase: grocery at one end and drug store at the other.

We arranged to meet again in another week after I had a chance to do a little due diligence. I discovered that his client's asking price was too high and, from other brokers, that he hadn't found much interest. Probably because one of his main leases was up for renewal and until that happened it was difficult to confirm a fair price.

When we met a week later the principal was there. I said I would pay his price but there were conditions. I explained to him my process. I put investor groups together and that it would take me at least 90 days to close. He said that was workable if I could give him a sizeable down payment. I had not a single investor in mind but had some ideas. I told him that if we could sign an agreement now, I could give him a very small down payment but would substantially increase it when and if his drug store renewed its lease which was about to expire. In my mind the worst that could happen was that I would only lose the small down payment if I couldn't raise the money. The property owner knew I was overpaying and might not be able to close but probably decided he would have a better argument to support his price in the future even if I failed to close. He could then say:

"We had a buyer at that price but his financing fell through."

My idea to raise the money was a long shot. I knew a very successful insurance salesman who had a strong client base of physicians. I explained to him the benefits for his clients to consider a private real estate deal. He was sold, particularly because I was going to share my fees, and he quickly lined up the investors. We were ready to go.

Two days before we were supposed to close, I was silently celebrating at the bar of my favorite neighborhood restaurant when the owner of the center spotted me and sat down next to me. He said:

"You know that center that you are supposed to buy in two days?"

"Yes, of course."

"Well someone set off a bomb in the drug store, you know the store that just renewed its lease, and its burned down. My partner just called me. The fire department is out there now."

We both got in the car and drove to the center. The inside of the drugstore was badly damaged but the structure of the center was fine.

We closed anyway. When the owner of the drugstore called me screaming that we were not moving fast enough, he had to start on his end of the repairs. I told him to forget it, read your lease. It is now terminated.

"Yes but we just elected to renew, we had an option."

"I understand but there is more than 50% damage and we are electing to terminate."

He knew what was really going on. We didn't want to be stuck with his small lease renewal increase. We wanted market rent. After some negotiation we got what we asked for and made money on the insurance settlement. My business was off and running. Four more shopping centers followed and three farmer home loan deals, small apartment projects in rural areas financed through the Department of Agriculture.

I moved to two other apartments over the next two years and eventually bought my first home, a new townhouse in a new subdivision in an older neighborhood. I had found a very contemporary house I liked better but was told that it was in a redlined neighborhood and I would have trouble getting financing. Of course that practice is illegal but was widely the way of the world in Cleveland. I put a sauna in the basement of the townhouse, built a new fireplace and wet bar, and found a tradesman to stucco the entire interior.

There were other changes. My parents had moved to Florida. Larry had a colectomy to finally deal with his colitis. He was working now and in fact had a great job. Although he never went to college he was employed as an electrical engineer in a new field that had something to do with microwaves. I found out years later he had lied about his credentials. The forged credentials never became an issue until many years later when an insurance check revealed the truth. They just changed Larry's title and were even more impressed than ever with his abilities knowing he was not formally educated. He was remarried now and doing great. Betsy seemed to have happily moved on.

I had arrived in what should have been a happy place. I was doing well, seeing the kids whenever I wanted, independent finally, out there dating a little and certainly not sleeping alone unless I wanted to, yet I was feeling incomplete and restless. I think with hindsight, I needed to be needed. I yearned for that codependent thing. And if you are looking for a human being to be your project it is never hard to find.

I had tried the disco scene, the neighborhood bar scene, the Quaalude scene, but never got close to finding someone I really felt I could share my heart with. I thought often of Kathrine but to my surprise she had married. A German guy from an old Nazi family that owned Volkswagen of Mexico among other things. I did meet up with her a couple of times over the years and tried to keep in touch by phone or email. Last year I learned that her husband had died and actually had another hidden family in Germany he never disclosed to her. Finally we fell out of touch. None of my emails were answered and old phone numbers didn't work. I found out why when I discovered her obituary on the internet. I wasn't even aware she was seriously ill.

I met a friend's sister who moved back to Cleveland after a bad experience with her boyfriend. It was a love story with a bad ending.

She was an inner city school teacher. I was very attracted to her and her story. We dated for a few months. I was happy with our relationship. She was not. I was a little sad about the rejection but she had flunked the Jamaica test so it would not have worked out between us. When, I took her to Jamaica she missed the magic looking for the absent disco.

I started a relationship with a waitress that proved sexually intense but intellectually stagnant. There are limits to great sex. Your first drink stimulates you, the second relaxes you and finally the third makes you want to go to sleep.

Every year I would go to the shopping center convention in Las Vegas to look for properties that I might buy. I never really got brave enough to buy something out of state but I did meet some of the famous real estate players. One of my Cleveland friends told me to be on the lookout for his old roommate from Kent State

university who lived in New York. He was working for Benedict Silverman one of the old New York shyster wheeler dealers. Lenny was a big guy with a big personality but didn't seem to understand how Benedict was screwing him. We had dinner and told college stories about our mutual friend. I had no clue at the time that he would play an important part in my life.

I am not sure what my kids thought was going on with me, and of course I could not know what their mother was saying, but I know they were relating to some of the part time women in my life. They loved the school teacher and had fun with the girl that set up a darkroom in my closet. At the time, it didn't appear that my role in their life was a plus or a negative. What's up with dad?

It's hard to be a divorced father. You have to get over the desire to try and prove you're better than whomever your mom is sleeping with and at the same time support your ex in her new life. Your kids are half of both of you whether you want to acknowledge it or not.

My youngest told me his friend's mom was really hot. I saw her shortly afterwards at a parent teacher conference and agreed. Hot. She worked in a flower shop next to a restaurant I visited weekly. I introduced myself and bought a large potted plant, which she said she would personally deliver. That started our relationship. Dating my son's best friend's mom proved too potentially dangerous and we ended it. It started up again much later.

In the early 80's Cleveland had begun to feel very small. The east side and west side had remained separate distinct worlds. Cleveland was a melting pot that didn't melt. The west side had its Poles and Russians, downtown was Black and the east side for me was where the Jews lived. It was becoming more and more obvious to me that my life, while now fairly successful, was quite small. Every day was a little more of the same. I became active in a Farmer Home Loan program that expanded my business to the very small rural areas of Ohio, but those were day trips and I still felt geographically constrained and intellectually stalled.

Things changed with one trip. On a whim I had taken a new love interest to New York to see a play. She was a stewardess I had met in Jamaica, who I particularly enjoyed since she had the ability to meet me anywhere with her own free ticket almost whenever I called. She had to fly out directly from New York to her hub in Atlanta after the play. I had free time in New York. I called Lenny.

● ●

CHAPTER 7: MANHATTAN

THE FIRST TIME I VISITED NEW YORK I was only eight years old. I don't remember anything about that trip except staying in a Times Square hotel where you could look out the window and see the Camel cigarette sign and smoke rings coming out of a smoker's mouth. I visited Manhattan a couple of other times while working for the law firm. One time I stayed at the Ritz Carlton and saw Bing Crosby in the lobby and Pierre Salinger in the elevator. But another time I stayed in a less famous hotel with a friend who picked up a street hooker who he took to the room we shared. I hid under the sheets while she was there but heard her say she could take out her teeth if he wanted the best blow job of his life. I wrote about it at the time as I recorded so many other events in my life that made an impact:

Street scene :
Lexington and 49th Street, evening lady at arranged price to come to Hotel room (2men to no involvement so far with straight person) to practice ancient art but first who must pass hotel john-arms who knows her art, who knows job could be lost but who also knows HERO from ice machine and also knows that Black man has few opportunities to fuck white woman ancient art artist for free and who knows life is cruel and who knows how to stand outside room 1602 while artist performs art to await and escort her to personal pleasure palace and then call patrons of hotel to make sure nothing stolen, who knows that HERO and FOOTBALL know that life has few opportunities to be big shot and knows that . . .
Difficult to ERECT when otherwise reasonable woman TAKES TEETH OUT . . . not to . . . not to be . . . not to be believed . . . close out degradation – close out day two.

DAY3: Exit empire state, exit bloomingdales, exit all the shit and candy samples of the whole world stuffed in too small _____. Enter Providence, Rhode Island.

I was not a fan of New York, but it was always fun for a day or two. My shopping center convention friend Lenny had been in

Cleveland visiting his old roommate John from Kent State. He insisted I say hello if I was in New York. He wanted to talk to me about his new company, Concord Assets.

Their idea was to buy a freestanding K Mart shopping center and apply a crazy tax structure to it that would generate enormous tax losses in the early years. They would allow an investor to pay for his partnership interest over a period of time staging payments to correspond with the tax losses generated. If you paid $25,000 in the first year you would get $50,000 in losses which you could apply against your ordinary income. If the investment was $100,000 you would pay over four years and sign a note for the rest which the company could discount at a bank. You would have the best of both worlds, a strong underlying asset and better than 2 to 1 losses.

The losses were generated by applying the rule of 78's to a mortgage. An outrageous idea. The rule of 78's is often used in a car loan so that the lender is rewarded if you pay off the loan early. Amortization of principle is delayed to the later part of the term. Interest is frontloaded. If you want to know the details check with Wikipedia. Applied to a mortgage of 30 years it generates tax losses on steroids. Concord Assets (the new company) had a "more likely than not" legal opinion from a very reputable New York law firm, only proving that with enough money any legal opinion is possible (buyable). (When this approach was ultimately challenged by the IRS Concord won but the judge confirmed it was "perverse but legal)." Lenny gave me the offering memorandum for the first deal and I returned to Cleveland and reviewed it with one of my accountant friends. He loved it and said he could recommend it to some of his clients. I actually sold out Lenny's first three deals in a few months and suddenly I was Concord's hero. The commission was large enough that if I shared, sales were easy. An ethical accountant would disclose the fee arrangement and he would act as an offeree representative. A less ethical one would not disclose the payment to his client. Their ethics should have been, but were not at the time, something I worried about.

It was legal. I could possibly be labeled a "pimp" but at the time I was not that hard on myself.

Lenny and his brother invited me to New York for the US Open in Queens. I had earned an obscene commission and they had a check for me. They were also trying to talk me into going to work for them. I knew that was a bad idea and quickly said no. I would never again be anyone's employee.

Later that weekend they talked about rolling out the program across the country. Lenny's girlfriend Sandy, who ultimately became his wife, was my new buddy. She was decorating their new apartment. The brothers were watching sports nonstop so I was ready to fly home. Sandy begged me to stay and go shopping with her. She had seen pictures of my condo in Cleveland and liked that style. We shopped and spent Lenny's money. Later she lobbied me to work for Concord. She told Lenny they needed Walter Cronkite to sell in the Midwest not Lenny Bruce.

"Please Richard, we need you. Someone a little less Jewish."

The deal I made with Concord allowed me to be hired as an independent contractor paid with an override fee on the gross sales of the company. Concord would provide an apartment in New York but I would only have to be there as needed. I could keep my condo in Cleveland and travel back and forth. Mostly I would be on the road for the company helping to close sales for the new salesmen, and be the "face" of the Company for formal presentations to broker dealers and accountants. If I had a title I don't remember it, but the salesmen knew I could help them make money so I was treated very well by all of them.

Finding a furnished apartment reasonably close to the company offices in the General Motors Building on 5th Ave. did not appear to be an easy task. There were few apartments to be had and I was put on a waiting list. In the interim they made a deal for me to have an extended stay in a mini suite at Le Parker Meridien on West 56th. I stayed there over six months before I moved to an apartment one block from Lincoln Center for the Performing Arts. The Meridien had a few interesting extras. Paul Schaffer of David Letterman fame seemed to show up every night to play piano and there was a bar on the main floor that attracted notables and high end escorts.

If you live in a hotel you eventually know the staff. I also knew the escorts, who would come to my room on occasion to shower. I never employed them or asked for a freebee. They did introduce me to a drug they seemed to love that was a white powder they snorted. Drugs scared me so I never really quizzed them about it or did it. I rediscovered cocaine later. None of these girls were trashy and all of them had other real jobs. The only notable I saw frequently during my stay was Dan Rather, who mastered walking through a room making eye contact with no one. Annie Lennox was alone with me in the elevator but out of respect and admiration, I employed the Dan Rather approach and made no eye contact with her.

My first week in the hotel corresponded with the Concord Christmas party. A day before the party Lenny said I had to skip the party and fly out to San Francisco to meet a broker who could potentially refer a lot of business. I called the guy to make arrangements. He said he was anxious to meet me but had decided to go to Cancun for Christmas. Could I meet him there?

So I spent Christmas with him in Cancun and he became a great source of clients. He didn't like Concord's deal much but liked to play tennis with me and hoped we could continue to meet periodically. Cancun did not live up to my expectations. It was essentially Miami Beach in Mexico.

I tried to hang in New York on the weekends, but most of the Concord people disappeared and I had too much alone time. Lenny and his brother stuck close to their high school buddies and played basketball or stayed in and watched sports. Concord's HR person asked me nicely but firmly to please not date any of the women in the office.

74

I discovered a profound loneliness in New York, particularly on the weekends. I lived in one of the nicest sections of Manhattan, had money in my pocket and a limo if I needed it, but spent most of my time walking the streets through a sea of strangers. In Cleveland, if you met someone new at a restaurant or bar you would probably see them again some other time. Not so in New York. I was a regular in most of the Columbus Avenue restaurants, met a few nice people but never saw them again. Of course I knew the bartenders and waitresses but they had their own social world.

I had a strange encounter with Robin Williams in a restaurant on Amsterdam street in Manhattan, but that had more to do with Cleveland than New York. A few years earlier Robin Williams and Chevy Chase were in Cleveland doing a benefit for Howard Metzenbaum, a liberal candidate running for the Senate. Robin was less well known at the time. He had been fixed up with a girlfriend of someone I was dating at the time. We had a double date and spent the evening in a Shaker Heights bar. Robin was very shy, almost incoherent and stoked with an assortment of drugs. Not a pleasant person to try and engage in a social light conversation.

But years later in an Amsterdam Road trendy restaurant I saw Robin having dinner with Robert DeNiro. I noticed Robin staring at me while I was eating at the bar alone. He seemed struggling to remember how he knew this guy at the bar. Apparently the light bulb went off and he mouthed to me "Cleveland" and then put his finger to his lips in the sign that says "tell no one."

I went everywhere alone in Manhattan and often escaped on the weekends to return to Cleveland and see the kids. If there had been a frequent flier program back then, I would still be traveling for free. This was pre-internet and pre-free long distance phone calls. I had a company calling card and encouraged the kids to call whenever they wanted using the code, but it was not the same as seeing them face to face.

I was living like a gypsy so there could be no long term relationship with a woman. I could, however, get laid. Alone in five star hotels with lots of cash seemed to make women traveling for business excited while they were also away from their real world and ready for a fantasy. Sex was becoming more and more impersonal and what I needed most was a hug from someone who really cared. I also needed someone to care about. To care for? Feeling sorry for myself I arranged a side trip to New Orleans to see Kathrine, who was now living there in one of her four homes.

Her husband was in Europe and I did my best to be respectful of their marriage, although I badly wanted to crawl back in bed with her. She took me to a new restaurant on Bourbon Street opened by an exciting new Chef Paul Prudhomme. I don't remember the name of the place but do recall you had to wait outside until they were ready for you and then share a large round table with a bunch of strangers. I was not impressed.

I flew directly from New Orleans to what was to become a summer stay in Houston, Texas, courting the east coast transplants that were swimming in money and consequently new prospects for us. Against all company policy I ended up sleeping with our Texas sales representative. I knew this was a bad idea but I felt for the single mom who desperately needed my help to sell a product she really didn't understand. I had never been to Texas and was amused by the zero lot lines and front yards of stone so different from the cowboy-movie expectation I had. The city's nightlife parallel worlds allowed you to choose between Travolta's Saturday Night Fever and/or Travolta's Urban Cowboy. Did you want to be a disco dancer or a cowboy on a mechanical bull? I wanted neither. I wanted to go home.

When I went back to my Cleveland home, it was difficult for me. It was hard to know what the kids thought of their dad who was never around. I knew I was not a traditional dad but hoped they still loved me. My attorney friends in Cleveland, now advancing their legal careers, were building a future but couldn't understand what my world

76

was like. I was always second guessing whether I wanted to return to the practice of law and a more normal existence.

After traveling to most of the major cities in the United States and watching Concord grow to one of the largest strip shopping center owners in the country, I was looking to do something different.

I rarely went to Concord's directors' meetings and avoided the office as much as possible. By now all the salesmen were smiling and dialing on the new power drug called cocaine and rapping in a talking speed frenzy. I couldn't deal with them when they were high.

I first tried this drug at a party Sandy gave. She opened a large powder puff and exposed this white powder, which she explained was the new miracle drug. It was the same stuff the escorts loved.

"Natives in Columbia have been chewing on coca leaves for centuries. It gives you energy without being addictive and there is no hangover."

As far as she knew it was also legal. We had all taken Dexedrine in college to cram for exams. This was like that. No big deal. I tried it with little response except my nose itched. I later learned that the restrooms stalls in New York has been refigured to insure privacy for snorting. Cocaine would not be a problem until much later.

The business meeting included a discussion of the West Coast market. According to their latest information tax shelter sales were booming on the West Coast and we were without salespeople there. We needed a West Coast office. Lenny and his brother both looked at me.

"Richard. Please. You have to do this for us."

"It will only take a few months."

It took two years. This became another hurry up and move. I had an apartment full of things in New York, even though it was a furnished apartment. I had bought a new TV and stereo and bedding and dishes, coffee machine, the usual kitchen stuff.

I packed my clothes and told the bellman I had an unusual goodbye tip for him. Take anything you want in the apartment. I'm out of here. Keep it for yourself or sell it.

CHAPTER 8: LOS ANGELES

MY FIRST CALIFORNIA HOME was in the Wyndham Hotel in Santa Monica, one block from the famous Santa Monica Pier. The Pier was built in the early 1900's as a way to transport Santa Monica's sewage into the ocean. Instead of wood they used concrete, which made it a national curiosity. Not such a good idea since it collapsed in 1919 because of rust. Once repaired it hosted the Whirlwind Dipper roller coaster and the largest ballroom in the world. The coaster disappeared but the ballroom lasted thru the Depression. The Pier suffered many failed partial repair attempts until finally in 1983 storms destroyed most of it. When I arrived it was mostly a memory and not restored to its present state until after I had left California.

I never thought of California as a fresh start. It was just another chapter in a life blowing in the wind. I wasn't excited to be in California or upset to be in California. I was simply numb. But I had a job to do and no advance team. I had to find an office location, find a place to live and hire employees for the office. I had a hotel suite, a suitcase, and a rented Lincoln town car that liked to slide through intersections on rainy days.

Someone in the New York office suggested I meet up with a guy who could get me a better deal in the Twin Towers in Century City, the "high end" prestigious part of the west side of Los Angeles. Century City was built on the former backlot of 20th Century Fox. The Towers housed some of the most important law firms and accountants in the city. I needed a "high end" building to sustain our image. The New York friend referred showed up with his extremely attractive wife at my hotel and promised me a great deal on a sublet in the Towers at approximately 20% less than the going rate. Forever suspicious, the next day I went to the manager of the building and discovered that I could make a better deal on my own. I learned later the attractive "wife" I had met earlier was actually a hired actress/escort to hook me into further "good deals." You just got to love LA.

Concord had great credit and a home office in an "A" building in New York. Credit plus credibility. Novel for LA. I would have an office in less than three weeks and it would be furnished from most of what was sold to me from the prior tenant.

I wanted to get out of the hotel as quickly as possible and was willing to overpay if necessary for a place to live. I would have been willing to move into an apartment but I preferred to find something furnished because I didn't expect to be there that long. Six months at most. I saw an advertisement for a condominium for rent in Brentwood (near where OJ killed his wife) but when I got there the very formal Persian (not yet called Iranian) manager said it was rented, not furnished and off the market. I asked him if he knew of any furnished condos for rent. He did not. After much haggling and five one hundred dollar bills I made a deal with the manager to rent the model suit month to month. I agreed to pay for a maid so it would always be available for sale. I moved in immediately.

The company that had occupied my new office and was moving out of state had a secretary I was able to hire. She was from South Africa and proved to be invaluable. She knew how to do everything I did not and handled all the mechanics of getting us up and running, including necessary paper work for the building manager. Employees also fell in my lap courtesy of a New York salesman, Adam, who was moving back home to LA. He became my right hand man and brought to our office three of his bond trader friends looking for a new opportunity.

My first attempt to establish a business relationship with an established source was not encouraging. I met with a senior partner of a prestigious law firm. He told me:

"I like your deal but we need to see if you are still around after a year."

"We have a lot of tax shelter guys operating out of the trunk of their cars that have given your business a bad name."

"You guys are probably different but strike one, you're from New York, strike two your legal opinion is not from our firm, and I'll hold off strike three if you are still in your office next year."

"If you are still here we'd love to talk again."

So much for my $50 lunch. If we were going to sell, it would be the hard way, direct "one on one" to clients. That would not be as easy and certainly not quick. Actually it would take over nine months to get sales rolling.

My Adam said I needed to buy a car and stop driving the pathetic Lincoln Town "scar."

I said I was not a car guy: "You buy it for me".

He did and I became the proud owner of a 300SD Diesel Mercedes, which I would keep more than ten years.

I managed to escape the LA scene since I was fairly consumed with work. I didn't date and only occasionally went out to the "happening spot." Usually after work I would have a drink in the building's bar, which often featured regulars like David Hemmings and the Ben Casey guy Vince Edwards. Hemmings starred in Michelangelo Antonioni's Blow Up and was now directing TV in LA. He had a larger than life personality and stories. Vince Edwards was more of a mystery and kept to himself.

One night I did go out and something very strange happened. There was a trendy restaurant bar in Brentwood that my new friend, the manager of my building, liked. She encouraged me to join her husband on a Thursday night which was supposedly the singles night.

I arrived a little early directly from the office, probably over dressed in a suit and tie, to discover there was already a line out the door. I would have never waited but arrangements had supposedly already been made and I had no idea the name used for a reservation. The girl in the line in front of me was also dressed for a dinner party and a little more fashionably attired than the other girls. She had an extraordinary figure. I couldn't see her face.

I heard her say to know one in particular:

"What do they think this place is, Studio 54?"

I responded from behind her shoulder:

"Actually there are no more lines at Studio 54. I guess it has already seen its day."

She turned around briefly checked me out as I did her. Her front was even more beautiful than her back.

"Are you from New York?"

"Yup. I just recently moved here."

That was all of it. There was no more small talk. The door opened and they let our section of the line into the restaurant. I ordered a drink and the beautiful girl in the line disappeared. About ten minutes later my friends arrived and we had dinner. After the dessert and well into the coffee phase, the girl from the line reappeared at our table and asked me if she could talk to me for a moment.

"You seem like a nice guy. My girlfriend was supposed to meet me here and she never showed up. I got a ride here and now I need a ride home. It's not far. Is there any way I can ask you to give me a ride home?"

I said: "Of course. I would be happy to."

She stood there while I said goodbyes and then she walked out with me. I did not valet and parked in the lot. About half way to my car, she grabbed my shoulder and started to fall. As I held her it was clear she was passing out. I picked her up and carried her to my car and put her in the front seat. I waited in the lot a few minutes to see

82

if she would wake up. Her breathing was not irregular. I thought she was okay but I debated what to do with her. Should I take her to the emergency room? Ultimately I took her to my apartment which was less than one mile away. Still passed out I carried her into the bedroom and dropped her on my bed. Soon she appeared to be lightly snoring.

In the living room I opened her purse and took out her driver's license and wrote down her name and address. Later, this proved to be an excellent move.

About a half hour later I went back to the bedroom and shook her arm lightly to try and wake her. She opened her eyes, and looked at me.

"Where am I?"

"You passed out on the way to my car. I wasn't sure what to do so I brought you here to my apartment. Are you ready to go home now? Do you feel better? Would you like to go to urgent care?"

"No, no…just give me a few more minutes to sleep and then please take me home." With that and completely unexpected she, in one motion, took off her dress and now lay mostly naked in my bed.

I am a gentleman but also human. I was aroused. She was truly astoundingly beautiful. I covered her with the blanket and made myself some coffee. I read the day's mail, looked at the paper and then tried again to wake her.

This time there was no problem. She said she was fine and would get ready to go and thanked me again. I closed the door waiting for her to dress and drove her home. I expected an apartment building but arrived instead at a very beautiful townhouse.

"Please come in. I owe you a nightcap."

I complemented her on her fabulous townhouse and asked her what she did. She said she was a model.

I thought: "Oh sure aren't they all."

She said: "I know what you are thinking, model/escort. No actually I have been very lucky with my career until recently. Let me show you my portfolio."

What I expected to see was your typical stock photos that most models have accumulated from decent photographers over the years. An assortment of poses. That was not what I found. Instead there were page after page of magazine advertisements featuring my new friend attached to overpriced high end consumer goods aimed at the glamour crowd. She was hawking everything from perfume to a Bentley. But the advertisement that most impressed me was the one for Black Velvet Whiskey where our girl is lying on her side on a couch in a black dress caressing a bottle of Black Velvet. The Black Velvet girl is a big time gig shared in the past by Cybill Shepherd, Cheryl Tiegs and Christie Brinkley.

"I'm impressed, you look amazing in these pictures."

"Thank you. I'm trying to look alluring. Ironic since I am no longer a sexual being. If you had ideas about a hot evening, I truly am sorry. You are the kind of guy I'd love to sleep with but for the moment my only lover has been heroin. Just a bad result of a failed relationship with an airline pilot I hope you never have to fly with. I'm on methadone but I have a way to go."

"Please don't go home yet. It is really late just come to bed with me. You can leave in the morning. We both need some rest."

Minutes later I was asleep. But after what seemed only a few minutes I awoke to noise downstairs. Someone else, a male voice, was in the house. I quickly got dressed and was grabbing my keys when my new friend appeared.

"Sorry about that. Just a friend I'm working with."

"That's OK I'm up so I might as well take off now. Good luck with everything."

I couldn't get out of there fast enough suspecting that her friend was her drug dealer and maybe this would be the unlucky night that life said goodbye to her. I didn't want to be around for that.

In the morning when I forced myself out of bed to start the coffee I realized that my wallet was not on my nightstand nor was my watch. In fact I remembered I left them at my models house. Luckily I had her name and address. I didn't expect to find her in the phone book but this was pre-cell phones and many people were still listed.

She answered. Felt bad. My things would be under her door mat.

I retrieved my stuff and never saw her again.

Months later I thought of calling her but didn't want to find out if she had lost her fight with smack.

It occurred to me that my father's famous college roommate, Jerome Lawrence the playwright lived in Malibu. Although he was the author of several books and plays, by far his most famous offering was Inherit the Wind, about the Scopes trial. I decided that just for the hell of it I would try to call him and introduce myself. After some searching I reached his secretary and a few days later he called me and to my surprise invited me to dinner at his home.

I easily found Pacific Skyway Lane, Jerry's street but had much more difficulty finding the house. At the street level there was little to see. The house was little more than a doorstep. After you reached the entrance, the house snaked down the mountain to reveal a steel and glass palace over ten thousand square feet. Nature usually hates artificial structures in California. Houses on stilts fall in the ocean. In the mountains, houses slide in heavy rain with the mud in monstrous heaps. That was unlikely for Jerry's house which was anchored to the mountain with huge steel braces and concrete retaining walls.

I dressed for the evening in my best non lawyer-like suit, a conscious attempt on my part to show respect for one of my father's friends. Jerry was in his seventies and I expected he'd be dressed.

I rang the doorbell plus intercom and identified myself to a voice that sounded like something from a McDonald's to go window. I fully expected a butler to open the door. Instead it was Jerry who inspected me as one might a new garden statute and then gave me a bear hug.

"My god, Richie, you look wonderful. But nothing like your Mom or Dad. I'll have to ask your Dad if Mom was busy with the milkman."

Jerry Lawrence aka Schwartz his real name, was dressed in a purple warm up outfit with Michael Jordan track shoes that had obviously never been used for running. He reminded me of the British guy that hosted family feud. Richard something, but not British. Maybe an American who had spent a lot of time there. Jerry had a large head and thick white hair cut short and combed forward in the front to rival Caesar. It was difficult to really "take him all in" at first because his eyes so riveted mine that to glance away would be obviously impolite. He had blue eyes that had not lost much power with age and still moved rapidly when he spoke

"Before we forget and do another thing you must sign my guest book."

As Jerry directed me to the stainless steel pedestal which held the book, much like the wooden ones do at funeral homes, I heard a door slam. Jerry noticeably flinched and slightly wrinkled his brow and then quickly recovered to walk me to a large terrace that overlooked Malibu Beach and consequently the Pacific. The requisite telescope was in place and it was not aimed at the stars but rather the beach.

"I like to do a bit of people watching to keep up with the latest fashions."

He kind of winked a dirty old man wink.

"My God, how rude of me. Would you like a drink?"

Jerry leaped away with a childlike giggle. Somewhere from the 10,000 square feet the chorus plays two more door slams.

"So Richie, your father tells me you're a big time lawyer with a wife and kids in the suburbs of beautiful Shaker Heights. Right."

"Actually, Jerry, I've been divorced now for a few years and no longer practice law. I'm in the real estate business. I do appreciate my father's gushing admiration. He always wanted to be a lawyer and so loves to talk about his son the lawyer."

"I see. Is there anything I can do to help?" As in "is this the purpose of this visit?" I laugh:

"No, if we run out of vodka you can buy some more."

Another door slam. This time Jerry stands up and removes his warm up jacket to reveal a pink "polo" shirt and releases his ample waist from jail by pulling his shirt from his pants reshoots his drink, and sits again with a release of air as if to lower the pressure of his body.

"Remember "My Fair Lady" Richie?"

"I'd be equally as willing for a dentist to be drilling as to ever let a woman in my life."

" Cyril Ritchard ?"

"He was one of many Professor Higgins who spoke the truth, eh? Applies to gay relations as well.

One final door slam. Jerry leaps up.

"Excuse me."

Shouting at no one in particular but apparently at the door slammer Jerry offers:

"Listen, you little faggot fucker, one more time and I'll throw you over this fucking mountain."

Jerry returns much relieved and very self-satisfied:

"I let this little 'putz' live with me while he's scoring one of my movies. He's got enormous talent but quite an attitude. I think he's jealous of you, Richie, or maybe just a little too strung out on that fucking cocaine he's always snorting. You're not a criminal lawyer are you Richie, or worse yet a narc?"

"Maybe", I joke. "But if I am, you're out of my jurisdiction."

"Go ahead, tell Bob and Jayne their famous Jerry is having a lovers quarrel. They wouldn't believe it. And if they don't, tell them Cole Porter had them as well and from what I hear he had a big basket."

"My composer friend is also the cook let me go get the brat."

Enter John Lennon if Lennon was alive and Jerry's lover and was twenty eight and if he had white hair and if he spoke like he had graduated from MIT.

"Richard, nice to meet you. I'm sorry I won't be able to stay for dinner but I'm not feeling well. I hate to let Mr. Lawrence down but sometimes these things happen."

Simultaneously with this little speech Jerry is mimicking the lovers speech and movements, much as Chevy Chase used to do on Saturday Night Live.

"I understand completely. Nice meeting you, goodnight."

Lover, composer exits stage left.

"Do you know how to cook Richie?"

"Fair, what do you have?"

Jerry opens the Subzero to reveal thin slices of pork already marinated.

"I hope you're a reform Jew. You eat pork?"

"Do you mean outside of Chinese food. Every Jew eats pork in Chinese food. Yes, I eat pork. Have any red wine?"

And then after dinner.

Everyone has been to a restaurant where stage pictures of stars line the walls-the pictures the publicity head of the studio releases complete with forged signatures. Jerry's office was different. Star A hugs Jerry alone. Star B hugs Jerry with his wife. Star C hugs Jerry with his toupee in his hand as a joke. Star D moons the camera. Director D and Jerry chew out a star. Jerry with the President. Jerry with the Chief Justice of the United States with the Prime Minister. Jerry with...

"You like my pictures?"

"Incredible."

"I've donated them all to Ohio State and they'll be on exhibit there starting in January. Hopefully I'll live long enough for some new pictures on the wall. Maybe my new friend Richie will send me a picture of himself and his kids."

"I'd be honored."

"So what do you want to know about your folks? They were young and beautiful. Lauren Becall and Cary Grant."

"Your dad had burdens I never had."

"What do you mean.?"

"He was normal. He wanted the normal things. To fit in with the world. Marry your mom. Be a success. Make a living. Have children."

"Why are those desires burdens?"

"Some of us, myself included, know we'll never fit in. We may have a talent. We may even end up with financial rewards but we're not normal and never will be. At least we cannot behave or think like most people. I never chose to be a writer. I never chose homosexuality. They are a part of me. I could never win in your dad's world. I had a free pass. I was allowed to be me. I accepted the fact early on that I could not be anyone else. I was never burdened by the potential of being normal by society's rules."

"Why do you pick the subjects you pick for your plays. Truth, justice and the American way?"

"I guess, it's because I like beautiful things. A clean simplicity. At its best that's what America is about. The truth, or at least the ability to seek it out."

"Hey, Richie, who did you say you married? Did I know her parents? Was she a Cleveland girl?"

"Yeah, Dr. Geller's daughter."

"Jac Geller?"

"That's the guy."

"God, was he handsome. I mean your Dad was good looking but Geller was fucking unbelievable."

He is silent while he visits another world in his memories.

"Richie, let's call it a night but I swear if you don't visit me again soon, I'm coming up to Cleveland and I'll explore your sex life and ask you all kinds of personal questions like what happened to your marriage."

"Jerry, thanks for everything. I will come see you again, I promise."

I never did see Jerry again. He died in 2004.

Still not having much luck at love, I decided the most reliable source was in Cleveland with my children and old friends. My townhouse was mostly empty since my visits were less frequent. I decided to rent it to a friend who had opened a restaurant. He traded guacamole, carna asada, and margueritas for his rent. It seemed a fair trade since my place was furnished and I didn't want it trashed and he was a quality tenant. My kids were doing better than I and seemed well adjusted and happy. I made arrangements with Betsy so the kids could spend part of their summer with me in California. I was excited to try and spoil them and impress them with my California life. Even though I was not happy I wanted to make sure they had a great time.

Since my place was not furnished and I had a month to month lease, it was easy to just say goodbye to my Persian landlord. He had a sweetheart deal with me and was not happy to see me go, but I had decided to move to the beach for the summer so the kids could have something to do that was better than sitting in restaurants with dad.

The place I found was in Marina Del Ray but not in the actual marina. Perpendicular to the beach was a series of streets named in alphabetical order for parts of a ship. I was moving to the T street. Topsail. The place was unfurnished. Really unfurnished. It had a stove but no refrigerator. It did have a sauna and underground parking to keep your car from being eaten by salt air.

I furnished the place with cheap but colorful furniture. I bought two single beds for the kids and a futon for myself. I put the futon directly on the floor and loved sleeping that way while I still had knees that worked in the morning. A short walk from my new home was Venice Beach and an assortment of interesting people. Some lifting weights, some drunk on roller skates, and one guy juggling chain saws. A little farther north and I was back where I started in California in Santa Monica.

There were downsides to living on a beach that belonged to God and the people. Anyone could walk on the strand in front of your doorsteps. I was on the first floor and subject to desperate women needing a bathroom and people who tried to U Turn on Topsail, only to find their rear wheels were now stuck in the sand. And then there were those that liked to drive to the end of Topsail late at night, with their car about twelve feet from my bedroom window and play their music too loud while they smoked weed or made love.

I was not making love and did not have a girlfriend. I was spending a lot of weekend time in nearby Hermosa Beach watching the drug and beach scene and roller skating with friends but I was still very solo. Sleeping alone was getting old. Things changed when one day weeks after the move, I asked my building manager friend if she played tennis. She did not.

"I think my bookkeeper does."

She shouts: "Lisa, you play tennis, don't you?"

Having a chance to leave her desk and stretch her legs, Lisa bolts up to announce that

"Yes, I am a tennis player".

"I will play a set or two with you. Whenever."

She was very cute wearing the tennis outfit but not much of a player.

Lisa was just a child in her early twenties with bright green eyes, dark hair, and legs that were too long for the upper part of her body. She walked like a little teenager who had not yet learned the technique of the graceful stride of a young woman. She was very bright with a bit of gosh and golly. And of course she was an accountant, not a bookkeeper, and if you're interested she had a boyfriend much older than her.

After our first tennis date, back at her tiny apartment, she announced that her boyfriend, who called her "popsicle toes," was no longer her boyfriend. She loved Michael Franks, though, so the nickname could stay and by the way since she no longer had a boyfriend, "You can make love to me if you want."

"No" she amended, "You cannot make love to me but you can fuck me if you want."

I should not have but I did.

Like the little girl she was, she loved to drive my new Mercedes and pretend to be a Hollywood star. I knew little of her family life except that she told me her dad was in a similar business to mine and that her mother was divorced from her dad and apparently an alcoholic.

A few days before the kids showed up for the summer, we met Muhammad Ali. I had seen other stars: Johnny Carson, Richard Dreyfuss, and the Happy Days cast when we took the kids to the television live taping. I never really responded as an excited fan. I actually saw too many Hollywood notables to mention here. A few I knew quite well. No one could compete with "The Greatest."

Lisa and I had played tennis and were in our tennis clothes when we drove past the Muhammad Ali gym. To my shock and surprise The Greatest was standing outside the gym surrounded by a ring of young kids. I pulled over as soon as I could and prepared to gawk. We had ice cream cones and of course were wearing tennis clothes and walked towards him. The tennis clothes were relevant only because Lisa's legs seemed to catch the attention of the champ. He made it obvious that he was staring at her, so I pretended like he was looking at the ice cream. I asked him if he wanted some ice cream, knowing full well the double entendre.

His response was to put up his arms in fighting mode and shout

"You calling me a nigger?"

Then he quickly smiled and laughed. I was too cool to ask for an autograph. But I will never forget the incident.

Lisa and my children got along very well. It was not surprising since she was a child herself. My kids took to the ocean and in fact the ocean early on took to them. It swallowed up their boogy boards and at least one time swallowed up their bathing suits. I took the kids up Highway 1 all the way to San Francisco where we visited Ghirardelli Square and all the tourist traps. The kids took a helicopter ride without me. Those things scared the hell out of me.

Later that summer we took a wild ride to Mexico with some friends. We bought the extra insurance to drive out of the country and headed down the Baja Peninsula in my new Mercedes to Ensenada. We stayed in a class D hotel where the kids discovered culture shock for the first time. They blew up their new boom-box by plugging it into the wall without a converter. Later with my friend, they managed to get arrested by the Mexican police by blowing up recently purchased firecrackers too close to their base. My Spanish speaking buddy saved the day by being able to smooth over the event. Thank God I was not with them at the time. I think they will never forget the trip. So much more happened there that they will never know about that reconfirmed my carelessness at the time. Thankfully we all made it home safe. And then after all the tourism, and when we were exhausted from too much everything, it was over and so was the summer. The kids would go back to Cleveland, and I knew in my heart I would have to return quickly as well. A long-distance father is hard to pull off. I knew after the summer I wasn't good at it. And I needed to get away from the sea of drugs that had invaded California. Cocaine was everywhere and it had begun to infect me.

I had told Lisa that my California tour of duty was about to be up.

"Let's just have fun, but you need to find another guy. Your boyfriend is too old for you. The Cleveland guy will be going home soon."

I should have said "in a week" because Lenny called and said we need you to go back to Cleveland and help sell in the Midwest immediately.

"California is under control."

I said: "I'll pack up the car and drive back. It will be an adventure."

He said: "No, fly back tomorrow. We will pack you up and put your car on a truck and it will all be there in less than a week."

Several weeks before, I had sent my parents tickets to visit. I missed them but it was also an act of ego. I wanted them to see that their son was doing well. I had been to visit them in their new condo in Florida and surprised my mom at Thanksgiving but I thought the long trip would be an adventure for them. Dad doing something other than playing golf.

I had hoped Jerry Lawrence was in town for a visit with my dad but he was in Europe so that wouldn't happen. My mom was horrified by my new beach digs and wondered if I had lost my sanity.

"Aren't you too old for this?"

I think my Dad liked it.

I wanted at least one dinner out to be a Hollywood experience. Hopefully they could spot a star or two. I took them to dinner to Mortons in Beverly Hills on a Monday night. From my many nights there I had become friends with the manager and learned that Monday night was reservation only for special people. You had better be famous or you weren't getting a table. I told him my parents would be in town and he loved the opportunity to help me entertain them. He made sure I had a good table at the best time on Monday.

Thankfully my Dad had left his golf clothes in Florida. No lime green sport coat. He had on a nice jacket and tie. My Mom of course was dressed for a party and looked beautiful. She had on her dancer legs and best high heels.

When we arrived I saw seated Ryan O'Neil and Farrah Fawcett, Carl Reiner, Richard Dreyfuss (always coked out) and a few others who were TV stars not yet on the A team. Johnny Carson usually came on Mondays but sadly was not there.

When we walked in and spotted my friend, the normal bar and restaurant hum was audible . When he walked us to our table like we were royalty the hum abruptly silenced. All eyes were on this couple. Is that Farley Granger? What is his name? They knew he was somebody and kept staring until they hoped to figure it out. My Dad remained totally unaware.

"Marvelous steak, Richard".

••

There was one last adventure weeks before I returned to Cleveland. Attending the shopping center Convention in Las Vegas as a representative of Concord Assets group was a significantly different experience from my earlier wanderings around the conference on my own. Concord had a bungalow behind the Desert Inn where we entertained sellers and future investors. I was involved with a constant meet and greet. In the evenings I went to sleep while my coworkers gambled and did the other things Vegas has to offer. I would rather take 10 friends out to dinner at an expensive restaurant than lose even one dollar gambling in Vegas. No table would be cheap enough for me. A dealer who beats you at blackjack five deals in a row requires too much restraint on my part. I was never a Vegas fan.

So the shopping center convention for me was just a lot of hard work and I was happy to return to LA. I left Friday afternoon. Saturday morning Lenny called me and said that they had the bungalow until Monday.

"Come on back, Rich. I need some company and I finally need some fun."

I didn't say no. I arrived late Saturday afternoon. We had an early dinner and then talked strategy for the evening. I voted for a Vegas show. Lenny wanted to gamble.

"You know, Rich, if I gamble I will lose at least ten grand. I have a better idea. Why don't I give you the money and you buy us hookers and cocaine until the money is gone?"

I had no experience with acquiring the entertainment Lenny requested in Vegas, but if you rented a private gondola at the Desert Inn in the 80's you had a concierge very different from that normally found at your Loews or Weston Hotel. If I wanted to hire Burt Parks to sing God Bless America in our living room, it could have been arranged.

So the first lady of the evening arrived shortly after my two ounces of cocaine. To say she was a lady would be accurate as to her gender but really she was just a kid. So many of the hookers in Vegas who were "higher quality" were actually college students just trying to make some extra money to pay for tuition. But if it were your daughter you would of course be horrified.

After the second girl arrived Lenny was ready for bed. What happened next surprised me and I was not easily surprised. Apparently the second girl had told her friends that some crazy guys had a ton of cocaine. The door was being knocked on and shortly there were at least 10 beautiful young girls who wanted to party. If not with Lenny or me, with each other.

Use your imagination.

Shortly after my Vegas trip my California tenure was over. There were goodbyes at my office party a few weeks later, and then I was gone as if I had never been there.

CHAPTER 9: BACK TO CLEVELAND

Wikipedia

*The U.S. Congress passed the **Tax Reform Act of 1986** (TRA) (Pub.L. 99–514, 100 Stat. 2085, enacted October 22, 1986) to simplify the income tax code, broaden the tax base and eliminate many tax shelters. Referred to as the second of the two "Reagan tax cuts" (the Kemp-Roth Tax Cut of 1981 being the first), the bill was also officially sponsored by Democrats, Richard Gephardt of Missouri in the House of Representatives and Bill Bradley of New Jersey in the Senate.*

By enacting 26 U.S.C. § 469 *(relating to limitations on deductions for passive activity losses and limitations on passive activity credits) to remove many* tax shelters, *especially for real estate investments, the Act significantly decreased the value of many such investments which had been held more for their tax-advantaged status than for their inherent profitability. This may have contributed to the end of the real estate boom of the early-to-mid 1980s as well as to the* savings and loan crisis.

After the Tax Reform Act of 1986 passed, I was out of business. Although I knew the law was coming, I managed to ignore the inevitable for a joyous year before it passed and instead concentrate on reintroducing myself to Cleveland. Soon I would be like the kid who was typing his answers to the bar exam when his ribbon broke. I would just sit there forgetting I had a pen.

I had let other friends live in my townhouse rent free for the last six months after my restaurant friend got his own place. They had not treated it well. Temporarily (as you will learn) I had a pile of money for something different in my housing options. Something big enough for my kids and their friends to visit.

I went house hunting with a real estate broker but found that most of the houses looked basically the same. I wanted something contemporary but nothing I saw excited me. When I was a young lawyer in a world of the lawyer uniform, button-down shirt, wingtips, Brooks Brothers three-button suit, the only way I could assert any independence was to dress differently. I discovered in Toronto, Canada a new approach to style, a place where men wore double-breasted suits and tie shoes that didn't look like you were going on a 10 day forced march for the army. I co-opted the Canadian style for myself, including a briefcase with a shoulder strap. And I wasn't gay.

I wanted a house that also reflected my sense of style and quickly realized my only option was to work with a blank slate I could remake. I finally found it in a suburb close to Chagrin Falls and the adjacent parks I admired. It was hidden in the woods on a three-acre lot. An old "A" frame. I loved it on sight but the problem was it was a wreck. I believe it started its life as a hunting lodge years before the suburb of Moreland Hills had single family homes and had been largely neglected since.

It had a natural septic system and a nearby creek and a rotting porch that surrounded the elevated house. This was not a house that a bank would take kindly to so I knew it would be a tough sell for the owner and that I would be able to get a great price by paying all cash. I intended to get a mortgage after I fixed it up.

I knew what I wanted it to look like but I didn't know any of the trades that could make my vision a reality. Betsy was friends with a decorator who had a look that wasn't mine. My grandmother would have used her Yiddish to described his look as ungapatchka. (Urban dictionary definition: "overly ornate, busy, ridiculously over-decorated, and garnished to the point of distaste)." But he knew the trades and was a ton of fun. Old ladies hired him for the constant party he offered as well as his limited decorating palate.

Paul liked me, which helped me persuade him to sign on. He was a gay man and we had mutual gay friends. I made a deal with him. I told him upfront that his style and mine were completely at odds.

"Beautiful, Paul, just not my kind of beautiful."

I needed him to coordinate the work on my house. He could charge his normal markup on labor and materials. I wasn't trying to beat him out of his fees, just compromise his ego. It had to be a "home by Richard home," not Paul. He agreed, convinced that I would give him full rein once he started. I didn't. He fought me the first day and then never again. I wanted the brick fireplace painted while. He said that was a horrible mistake. We fought and I reminded him again of our deal and then that was it. He complied and was a great help.

A retired shop teacher from Heights High School built the furniture in the master bedroom, which was upstairs where the loft overlooked the main room. The dresser and bed were fixed permanently into the walls. The fabric on the walls and blinds allowed the room to black out even in bright sunlight. All the lighting in the house was converted to halogen. The kitchen was torn apart and wooden cabinets were installed with modern appliances, Subzero refrigerator and a trash compactor. The high lofted ceiling was painted white and the floors sanded and pickled. The Israeli deck builders tore down the old deck that surrounded the home and rebuilt it in a few days with a choreographic display worthy of an old Hollywood movie.

I had a sauna built from scratch this time. The master sauna maker did not speak English but smiled a lot. The sauna in my townhouse never got hot enough so we used a larger heater. Anodized aluminum railings were installed around the stairways and deck.

Some of my favorite pieces of furniture in the house were acquired from the manager of the Cleveland Higbee store. The store was closing and I found some fabulous antique pieces in a Laura Ashley display. I asked the manager what would happen to the furniture when the store closed. He didn't know or care but if I wanted to buy it, all I had to do was make him an offer. I did. All cash and it was mine. I bought my couches in New York from Ligne Roset with Paul's decorator card and discount and had them shipped. I bought Paul's beautiful wooden dining room table to be used instead for my office desk downstairs in the room with the sauna. The other bedroom was more traditional and became my son Steven's room.

During the home rebuilding I had an unexpected house guest. But that is an entirely different story.

Lisa called from California to ask how everything was going on my return to Cleveland.

"How are the kids?"

It was a perfectly delightful conversation. I thought: Congratulations Richard, you ended a relationship successfully. You were still friends. But there was more.

"I have a few weeks' vacation due and wondered if you would mind a visitor for a few days."

Actually, I welcomed a "visit" since I had just distanced myself from a relationship that I suspected was becoming dangerous. I had been in an intense sexual relationship with a waitress who was morphing it into something more. I was not a welcome participant and it was becoming ugly. She was actually stalking me. Lisa would be a good buffer. And my kids would enjoy seeing her.

What I didn't know was that Lisa was not flying up as I had assumed but driving from California to Cleveland in her Ford Fiesta with most of her earthly possessions. I learned of this for the first time in a frantic phone call from Albuquerque, New Mexico. Lisa's car had become ill and she was stranded. Of course without considering all the consequences I told her to get a hotel room and await further instructions.

My next phone call to her told her the time I would arrive in New Mexico. I flew there, had her car fixed, (a one-day job,) and then stuffed myself into her little beast and drove Lisa and her things to Cleveland. Why didn't I drive her back to California? I don't know except it seemed like a step backward at the time and against the forward momentum of my life. Codependency seeking?

Lisa and I stayed in the new house during the renovations and while I was at work in my new office, she made it clear to everyone who would listen that this was her new house and that if there were questions about anything they should be directed to her. From the first day Lisa arrived, I plotted ways to get her to go home, but I learned she had quit her job and once again I felt stuck. Lisa's father called the house. I said Lisa was sleeping let me wake her. He said: "No, don't do that. Just tell her her mother died."

I thought this was incredibly callous. I learned later that her mother in her final days of alcoholism had checked into a hotel and drank herself to death. The entire mother, daughter, father alcoholism thing seemed so foreign to me. Who could of guessed I would understand this so much better in just a few years.

Months later I would pay for Lisa to move out into an apartment I found for her. She found a real estate job working for another friend and ultimately I helped find her a husband.

We both worked out at the same health club. There was a guy there that I knew had his eye on Lisa. I let him know Lisa and I were just friends (I didn't add, friends with benefits). Ultimately they would become "a thing" and get married. I was not invited to the wedding. I have never heard from or seen Lisa since.

What I did notice was that my pile of money was shrinking quickly. Concord's deals were over. They had moved on as a new public deal that I learned about at a sales meeting. They did not include me. Basically they were moving in another direction and I wasn't invited. I did have one last play with them.

They had over 300 K mart freestanding shopping centers that had only one tenant and no opportunity for increased income beyond K Mart's rent. The Concord boys knew about a tax structure but really had no idea about managing real estate. They had not even done a proper lease analysis of the centers.

In one week of 14-hour days in New York, I revamped their management department, reviewed all the leases, refined their budget, saved them a fortune, and introduced the parking lot kiosk idea which added a new stream of income to all the centers. You have seen the coffee and photo stores in parking lots. They had not.

That week cost them my income tax bill, which they happily paid. I had made them a new fortune but my Concord career was now officially over.

So that helped my bank account but then there was my father's disaster, Larry's divorce, and a nasty lawsuit.

In 1977 Williamson, West Virginia suffered the Great Flood. The Tug River, which separated downtown Williamson between two states West Virginia and Kentucky, reached levels that covered houses and

104

most of downtown. Damage was over $200 million and over 2000 people were left homeless. Flood insurance was impossible to get then and most businesses lost everything. Few reopened. The Schwachter building, which housed my dad's clothing store, the business he had inherited from his father and owned solely after buying out his sisters, completely flooded. My dad had already moved to Florida and my parents were running the business long distance. My dad flew to Cleveland and I went to Williamson with my dad as soon as the National Guard soldiers would let us in. When we arrived the waters had receded but everything, all the inventory had been soaked in the flood waters and there was structural damage to the building. I rented a truck and loaded it up with all the inventory, and drove the truck to Cincinnati, and had it all laundered at a coin-operated laundry. The clothes were all ruined from a commercial standpoint but clean and wearable. I drove back to Williamson with the cargo and my dad and I gave them free to families in need.

After four days of doing what we could we left. I had a new passenger to deliver to my mom. A three-week-old poodle puppy that had been promised out to a family that could no longer handle a new mouth to feed. The new arrival rode home with us. My mom happily took the dog.

Strip mining had helped speed the waters that stoked the flood. If you cut down the trees the water runs more swiftly off the mountains. Today the Corps of Engineers has protected the town with retaining walls. Back then the only relief was the SBA's government loan guarantees to reopen businesses. My dad was determined to reopen and got a loan. Years later I would learn that he had personally guaranteed his loan. The store reopened but never regained its former glory and closed. My dad would have been fine if he had just sold the building, paid off the loan balance, and walked off with the difference.

But when I returned to Cleveland from California he was excited about plans to convert the building into a bed and breakfast. Larry, who was now living in West Virginia and had been managing the store, and blamed unfairly for its loss of business, would supervise the reconstruction. No one was dumb enough to loan my dad the money except for his ego inflated son Richard. It took my dad exactly nine months to lose my entire college fund for both kids. Eventually I was able to sell the building "as is" to recover some of the loss, but so much for the now empty college fund.

I fared better with Larry's divorce. That only cost me $10,000 but years later when Larry died it cost me a six-month court battle over an insurance policy.

While I was in shock over the end of my tax shelter career, cocaine became a prominent part of my friends' daily entertainment. And part of mine. Cleveland was discovering the powder about the same time that California had grown tired of it. Paul had huge quantities that he wanted to hide from his boyfriend so he kept it in the crawl space in my bedroom behind the dresser drawers. Cocaine hurt my nose and dried out my eyes. Its only value to me was another ego fulfillment device. I had it for my friends and my friends liked to come over and play. My spirit was riding on empty.

I thought resuming a legal career might be an option so I became "Of Counsel" in a law firm downtown in the Terminal Tower, which was undergoing renovation. I would have to build a practice from scratch and after six months I hated the trip downtown and thought there must be other alternatives. Next stop was a guy who specialized in government housing, who proved to have an ego even greater than mine at the time. It couldn't work. That lasted three weeks. Another friend in the financial planning business wanted me and at his urging I actually became a Series 7 broker and got an insurance license. But we butted heads and I lasted a few more weeks there than at my previous effort.

I sold my townhouse, which I had rented out after my new house was built, and so I had a few more dollars in my stash to figure out my life. But I was adrift and had no woman in my life and little direction except for my new increased involvement with my kids. I was learning how to be a father. But unsettled and lonely-when along came Tamma.

CHAPTER 10 MEET TAMMA

IT STARTED IN A RESTAURANT. Not what you would think. Not late at night. Not "the place to be," just a restaurant that served a great burger and fries and a good pour after a hard game of racquet ball. I was there alone at a table. Not even sitting at the bar. There were only two girls at the bar and they were laughing and looked as if they had been friends since nursery school. The taller girl was very angular and quite attractive. The smaller girl was at first glance your typical Jewish yenta. We used to call them tits on sticks. Large breasts, no ass and skinny legs. And of course no "verbal holdback."

It went something like this: The smaller girl walks over to my table. Much cuter than I had noticed. Skin like a little china doll. I guessed mid 20's (she was 32).

"My girlfriend would like to meet you."

I respond: "That's it? No "Hello my name is---and my girlfriend would like to meet you."

She echoes: "OK, I'm Tamma. You know the rest."

"What about you. Don't you want to meet me?" I inquire.

"Tamma is already taken."

"Okay I get it, I'll meet your friend, but when Tamma is no longer taken, here is my card. Call me and we can have dinner."

Seven days later, about seven in the evening on a Saturday night, while I am getting ready for a date with a friend of a friend from out of town, I get a call.

"Hi. Tamma is no longer taken. I'll be over at nine."

And she was.

She wore the same dress she had on at the bar, drove some yellow car I had never seen before (I think it was a Plymouth Arrow), told me to tell my date "something came up" and didn't leave my side except for a few months until she died.

I was 16 years older than Tamma so, of course I felt blessed by her beauty, her youth, and her sexuality but those were not the things that lit the spark, the spark that almost killed me. There were other things. I used to be in shape and was a fairly decent long distance runner. I had begun again to see if I could restore my body to former greatness. I began with painful short runs, jogging in my immediate neighborhood and in the park just steps away.

Tamma smoked so many Winston Ultra Lights that I almost never saw her without one lit. We bought them by the carton, never the pack. One day, in the first week of her stay, after I discovered she did at least have a place to live, (the basement of her girlfriend's house) she said that my running thing was pathetic and would end poorly with a back problem to supplement my knee problem. That her brother ran marathons and was quite good but would no doubt end up crippled from it as well.

I responded that with all those cigarettes she wouldn't make it a hundred yards. That was why she was putting running down. She went to her car and laced up some yellow high-tops that had Tweety Bird and Sylvester on their sides and said" Let's go, big boy." And ran me into the ground.

Sometimes I'd catch her reading one of my books. Not the classics but not Patterson. She didn't know I was watching. She would sit in a yoga like thing with her legs all tucked and the book in one hand and the cigarette in the other and I would watch the pages fly. Was she really reading or just turning the pages? She could read an entire book in a few hours and later, knowing that she had not seen me spying on her, I'd ask her if she ever read the book I saw her reading. She'd answer, "Of course," and then answer all my questions. No one could read that fast. She could.

Her hair covered her beautiful face and so I suggested she would look even more beautiful if she cut her hair short. It wasn't like I was Professor Henry Higgins attempting to remake her in some more upscale image. I just thought she might like a change and a chance to have her hair cut by an upscale salon. So with some reluctance she agreed and marched off with me to the joint that cut my hair. They were expensive but I loved the people there and did not feel threatened in the least by the "metro man" image I was beginning to cultivate. Nice haircut. Nice clothes.

So fearless Tamma, who usually had a running verbal banter, was suddenly silent as she sat in the boss's chair and prepared herself to have her hair cut short. As he cut the first strand the first tear leaked, followed by the second. No actual crying, but at the conclusion, she studied herself for some time and then collected herself, I think with an awareness she probably never before had and announced:

"Damn, I look good. Okay I'll let you buy me a few new clothes if you really still want to."

She had never really had anything nice, and was fascinated to shop in a higher end store. I suggested that a few wonderful understated things were better than a closet full of crap. She was a good student except for shoes, where it was hard for her to abandon the "fuck me" style that girls were wearing for something a bit more reasonable.

Until the end, she never bought an article of clothing without me. She trusted herself in all things but not clothes. The truth was she looked great in anything she put on.

The only other act of change, I worked on Tamma was not done in a store. She worked for a securities broker who represented some of the richest people in town. He was brilliant but without morals. He had several mistresses and once told me he'd never run out of people he could cheat. He was right.

Tamma did all his dirt, which meant basically that she handled all the calls from the clients who wanted anything other than to buy stock and she did all the bookkeeping and record keeping, which was a substantial effort since computers were just starting to actually assist us a little but not much. Her boss truly appreciated her abilities but never rewarded her financially and she needed the job and needed to put up with his shit.

One day I picked her up for lunch, and she discovered that not only did her boss know me but that he fawned all over me. Obviously, after that, she somehow felt less intimidated by him and more comfortable at work.

I am not exactly sure how much time passed before Tamma asked if she could invite her family over for dinner. We had gone on a trip together to Mexico where she briefly described them. She had met my folks on a trip to Florida, so it seemed timely to finally "meet and greet" hers in person. They lived in an apartment complex only a few miles away.

Tamma had grown up in the same city as I, although I went to the upscale rich people public high school while she was one of only a few white kids in her high school.

I had a "gay" housekeeper who was not happy with her because she expected him to work. Pre-Tamma he did a little "straightening" and talked on the phone most of the day to his boyfriend who was a Marine recruiter. (I'm not making this up). I suggested to her that he could cook dinner for her family. Tamma said "No, I will take care of it myself." I offered that "we could grill out and I would make steaks" when she surprised me with: "That wouldn't work because we were going to have at least 30 people and I'll do the cooking." Well Okay.

We usually ate most meals out and Tamma never really expressed any interest in food other than sushi. I certainly didn't know she knew how to cook. But then she was the oldest of four kids and her Mom was not functioning when she was young (she was schizophrenic) and dad worked (tool and dye shop), so she basically raised her two brothers and sister on food stamps and wits. Of course she could cook.

When her mom walked in the door, it was clear Tamma was a combo child. A little of mom and a lot of dad. Mom's brain and maybe her feet and hands; the rest was dad.

You could tell that mom was once beautiful but now had a bit of that post shock-treatment look. Eyes not quite focusing as if the last acid trip was a little too intense. (Actually grandma, who was also there, I later learned, had received over 100 shock treatments in an attempt to regain her sanity.) Grandmother's sanity was clearly intact. She was doing her best to market her granddaughter to me.

Dad looked a lot like Ichabod Crane of Sleepy Hollow fame. In fact, if you get hold of the Norman Rockwell version you can see his exact likeness. Tamma inherited his skinny legs and small head.

Her oldest brother was a younger version of dad and her youngest brother a male mom. Tamma's youngest sister was a dead ringer for the comedian Sandra Bernhardt, (the comedian and Madonna buddy).

Grandma was with her third husband who she had picked up at a bus stop. This husband, who was the nicest in the whole crowd, was an heir to an underwear fortune but had managed to spend and lose most of his money. Grandma, the story goes, was waiting at a bus stop in Woodstock, New York when the poor fool happened by. Grandma flagged him down and never let go until he married her. Sounds familiar. Grandma's first husband, the father of Tamma's mom, was an expert at bankruptcy fraud and had apparently sexually abused Tamma's mother.

The essence of his bankruptcy scam was to buy a business for more than it was worth with a little cash and a big note, and then sell off the inventory and fixtures for cash and default on the note declaring bankruptcy. Nice guy. Apparently he tried to abuse Tamma but she kicked the be-jesus out of him.

Tamma's mother's sister was there with her children. I won't elaborate too much here but Tamma's aunt was a distorted version of her mother. All the features had bled and spread. What was left was

112

like plastic surgery gone awry. The uncle, who serviced vending machines, spoke in mono-syllables but seemed nice enough and earned points for sticking with his wife. His son has there. He was either Paul Bunyan or the ox but also a nice guy.

Some friends of the family somehow decided they were invited as well and made themselves at home. Tamma cooked pork filets in a red wine sauce and a host of other appetizers new to my palate but excellent. She did a great job for a beer crowd. What was disturbing about the "meet and greet" was the feeling that this crowd had a secret. That somehow I was the butt of a joke. I felt a little like Rosemary in the movie Rosemary's Baby. Did they have something evil in store for me?

Tamma surprised me by understanding the basics of tax shelters. She also knew more about investment alternatives and the stock market than I did. I was the Series 7 broker but she had hands on experience and actually knew how to book trades and work the arcane broker devices used in the 80's. She asked me why I wasn't back in the real estate business if that had worked for me before. The answer again related to the kid whose ribbon broke typing during the bar exam. Tamma was right, I needed to get back in the game.

My investor group was now busy buying office buildings with my former partner who had helped me raise the initial Concord money. I decided that to restore my reputation in the "real" real estate world, not the tax shelter hybrid real estate world, I had to "go one alone" without investors.

A friend of mine who was also a broker suggested I consider apartment buildings in Shaker Square. There were two buildings that came as a set containing over 200 units. Shaker Square was a combination of three basic groups: the gay, the elderly, the professionals. After I was divorced for a short period I lived in the gay part on the west side of the Square. I had no idea at the time that it was the gay side until I had lived there for over a year and other tenants in the building invited me to enough parties that made it clear. The buildings I was considering were in the professional and seniors categories. They were owned by a guy of shady reputation, and although I bargained for a fair price I didn't do enough homework.

I pretty much emptied my wallet and pushed every last dollar on the table to buy the buildings. Each month I barely met expenses. The trick was to own it long enough to slowly increase the rents without losing too many tenants to the increases and spending too much on improvements and repairs. I had to compete with other rentals across the street in Cleveland where the property taxes were lower than Shaker, but I had to buy my water from the City of Cleveland. And then the City of Cleveland surprised me with an unpaid and undisclosed $50,000 back water bill. I resolved this with the help of a good political friend and a bottle of single malt scotch. A bigger problem remained with the 24/7 payroll required to run the all night indoor garage. Since there were not enough parking spaces for everyone to park inside the building, and everyone wanted to park inside particularly in the winter, there needed to be a 24/7 attendant to jockey cars if necessary in the middle of the night. This burdensome addition to payroll could have been resolved if I was not in shock from the delicate balance between the income and expenses in the building. There were solutions I was not creative enough at the time to consider. I could have offered reduced rent to some tenants to park outside, but I was no longer thinking clearly.

In a short time Steven was living with me, while Marc stayed with his mother and Jon. My attempt at normalcy would have been easier if I hadn't developed three herniated discs in my back. Steven managed to run an all-terrain vehicle I owned into a tree and needed serious face stitching, but overall there was peace with the kids and Betsy.

Tamma and I grew closer and more comfortable. Our social routine did involve lots of eating out and some drug use but we had a large group of friends and life finally seemed normal. The apartment ownership business, however, got complicated when I suspected and later confirmed that my on-site manager was stealing from me. But I had already decided the apartment was too much for my cash reserves

In addition, Steven was going to college and the money that was saved for that got blown up in the Williamson flood disaster. So the buildings got sold and Steven went off to college.

Desperate for a new business as far away from real estate as possible, I bought part of a stun gun company owned by a Shaker policeman and a lawyer friend. What was I thinking? When it became time for Marc to go to college it became clear to me that if I was going to pay for two kids in college at the same time my, house had to go. With a few tears I said goodbye to my A frame.

Rhonda was my secretary years ago when I worked with Herb and remained my friend throughout her short life. I loved her for her honesty and compassion. I had few friends that I could confide in and cry to. She was my closest female friend. Tamma exceled at knowing the difference between shit and shineola and from the start suggested the stun gun idea was not going to work. But by then I was doubting her judgment since she was losing interest in working and drinking much more and using drugs regularly. Our friends were calling her Marni for her interest in Grand Marnier after already having too many vodkas with dinner. I told Tamma to tone it down. She'd smile at me and respond in her best New York Jewish accent:

"Ok, I better be good, or else! Who would have a girl such as myself?"

She was right about the stun guns. They were too controversial back then and the laws controlling this type of device were uncertain.

One night while partying at our favorite steak joint, Tamma and Rhonda introduced me to Andy. Andy was the poster boy for what you hoped your Jewish son would become. He had been working for the A ranked law firm in Cleveland and was a handsome, eligible bachelor on the east side of Cleveland.

Andy had an idea for a business as did I and we opened an office together to try and make both work. They were two good ideas but ultimately failed and set the stage for my move to Florida.

From the time our new business started until the time Tamma and I left for Florida, we lived in three new residences. After we sold the A frame, the thought of moving into a standard apartment building was too much of a slide to the bottom. Instead we moved into Herrick Mews an old Cleveland landmark not far from where my grandfather Deutsch's home had been. Mews are old stables that have been converted into housing. Once Marc was accepted into medical school we moved to another apartment closer to the Medical School so Marc could live with us. It was on the third floor of an old but beautiful apartment building and required strong knees since it had no elevator. The woman directly below us held house concerts in her apartment and we enjoyed free concert quality classical music weekly. On Occasion we were able to feed Marc's classmates and actually let Tamma's sister live with us part time.

Eventually we moved to our last Cleveland home in Chagrin Falls and rented the penthouse overlooking the city in an area that used to house the TB hospital when higher altitudes were part of the cure.

Andy's business idea was Smart Health Plus, a discount card you could buy that gave you pharmacy and dental discounts. We were undercapitalized and before our time. Similar concepts have since been successful particularly with regard to dental discounts. We sold the idea to a guy who traded television equipment for massive commercial airtime, and planned to flood the airways with commercials for the card. He actually used Betsy in one commercial but I don't think he made a success of the card either.

My business idea was more complex. If you developed certain government subsidized housing projects, you were required to maintain reserves called "residual receipts and replacement reserves". Over the years these reserves became substantial, but distributions were restricted by the rules and HUD only allowed a limited range of investment for these funds. The income on the reserves was taxable, although the funds could not be distributed. Most of these funds were held by mortgage companies and offered no benefit to the actual investment owners of the properties. Property owners were happy to

116

pull these funds away from the mortgage companies and invest them privately if this was permissible. They also wanted to stick the middle finger to the mortgage companies if they could.

With the help of a Cincinnati company, Andy and I developed a mutual fund to invest these funds in a more profitable manor for the owners but still consistent with HUD rules. The Freedom of Information Act provided me with the names of all the property owners affected and I began to pitch them with some success.

When the details of what we were trying to do became widely known, the mortgage companies went nuts and did all they could to stop us. They eventually lobbied HUD to change its rules and put us out of business. We were finished. At least it was an intelligent, novel effort.

Three events then converged to send Tamma and me on our way to Florida. The first occurred while Steven and I visited my dad on his 80th birthday. Mom had arranged a party for their friends and a few relatives including, dad's sister and her husband. About an hour into the party my dad confided in me that he didn't know most of the people at the party. He was unusually quiet that night. Shortly after the party he was diagnosed with the first stage of Alzheimer's disease.

Months later I moved to Florida to help out. When my mom initially told me dad was diagnosed with Alzheimer's disease I argued with her.

"How do you know? Has he been properly diagnosed, by a neurologist, in addition to the family doctor?'

"Of course. Take him yourself if you want and ask the doctor anything you want."

I did take him to the same neurologist my mom had already seen. I wanted my own Q & A opportunity. The doctor remembered my dad and did not look happy to see me or him.

Dad sat on the examining table and smiled at me, looking handsome as ever. When the doctor shined his light in my dad's eyes my dad punched the doctor hard in the face. Diagnosis confirmed.

The second event was a visit from one of the Concord officers, David, who had a business proposition for me if I moved to Florida. I respected David and considered him an ethical, intelligent, major force in Concord's success. He had recently been screwed over by Lenny and now was in business for himself.

The third event had something to do with Abe Lincoln's disease or more properly Marfan Syndrome. Quoting Wikipedia:

Marfan syndrome (MFS) *is a genetic disorder of the connective tissue. The degree to which people are affected varies. People with Marfan tend to be tall, and thin, with long arms, legs, fingers and toes. They also typically have flexible joints and scoliosis. The most serious complications involve the heart and aorta with an increased risk of mitral valve prolapse and aortic aneurysm.*

Rhonda had cautioned me about her brother Steven. He was according to her "a bit of a snake". He was a gay lawyer specializing in divorce, who somehow had inherited a bundle from a client under suspicious circumstances. Rhonda and Steven had lost their mother, whom I had met when Rhonda worked for me, to a sudden heart attack. They had also lost Steven's twin sister to a motorcycle accident.

When Steven met Tamma for the first time he was shocked by how much he felt she resembled his late mother. Rhonda agreed. He was fascinated by her. Tamma loved Steven's new attention and his ongoing party stoked by alcohol and drugs, which complemented her present temperament.

Steven's doctor in Florida suspected he might have Marfan's Syndrome. There was no direct test for this syndrome but it was called Abe Lincoln disease because a common profile was someone with extremely long arms and fingers. Steven flew to Cleveland to get another opinion from the Cleveland Clinic. I accompanied him, where they confirmed the diagnosis and scheduled Steven for open heart surgery to avoid his heart valves from splitting apart. It was suggested that maybe Marfan Disease had been the cause of his mother's death.

Steven and his gay friend entourage came to Cleveland for the surgery and he then rehabbed at our apartment in Chagrin Falls. It was then that he reciprocated by offering us to stay with him in Florida until we found our own place.

The fact that Tamma now had an adoring friend made the move more attractive to her than before.

Tamma became unexpectedly pregnant. I was not thrilled but assured her that I would support any decision she made about continuing her pregnancy. She decided not to have the child. I am not sure what her thought process in making the decision actually was but I believe the abortion contributed in subtle ways to her decline. I think the procedure popped the imaginary bubble she had of a normal life. She was not going to be a mother, she was not going to be a career woman and she was no longer going to be the sole grownup in her parents' and siblings' life. Instead she would float without responsibilities and escape to the bizarre world of a Florida beach party.

One of our high priced physician friends performed the procedure in the hospital, costing about 20 times what it would have cost at a clinic, but I felt guilty knowing in my heart of hearts I didn't want the responsibility of raising another child. I wasn't that good at raising the ones I already had.

I needed to go to Florida but not for the party. I didn't trust Steven and didn't like his influence on Tamma, but then wasn't I also sliding down the tubes? Weren't my glory days over? Did my kids really need me anymore? I couldn't consult with my brother because Larry was gone. Cancer took him and I wasn't there by his side at the end. I felt very guilty that I had not made it to Florida before he died. Was all my love and empathy bullshit? And did I really want to stay with this woman who was drinking more and looking forward to a party I was not sure I wanted to attend? A party to which I was not even sure I was invited. Was it guilt now or love that held us together? I didn't ask myself the right questions then because I really didn't want answers. I was frightened of the truth. And during my confusion, throwing all logic aside, Tamma and I got married and threw the party of the year.

Tamma was planning a party for my 50th birthday. As the plans escalated, half kidding she said that the party was getting so elaborate that maybe we should finally get married at the party, get double use from the event. I had no thoughts on marriage again. I felt like my life was going to hell, we're starting over in Florida, why the hell not. Tamma certainly wasn't marrying me for my money. I was almost broke.

But then fortune smiled on me. My restaurant friend had his own disaster when his trendy restaurant was suddenly empty because of road closures and massive road reconstruction that made casual trips to his restaurant impossible. He confided in me that he would have to close and go bankrupt. During our conversation I asked him about his lease, hadn't it just been renegotiated?

I discovered that his lease was assignable, very long term and actually now below market. I found a buyer for his restaurant within the month, largely because of the very valuable lease. Brad wanted to pay me in a trade.

The trade was the wedding reception.

We sent out our golden invitation tickets as if it were my birthday party. We had over 150 people invited, including my parents and some of their friends. Everyone showed up, including many who were not invited. As the guests arrived for my birthday, we were getting married in the hotel lobby. It was great to see my parents and their friends. I have a recording of the wedding and party on my computer. I don't have a recording of my mother berating me for a lavish party when I owed my dad so much money.

"Mom, I think dad has told it to you backwards. Can we discuss this some other time?"

My mom died believing I owed my dad hundreds of thousands of dollars. I never wanted to hurt her with the truth. Avoiding a fight with my mother as she approached ninety was worth a lot of money.

The Friday night wedding lasted until Sunday morning, when those that decided to book hotel rooms finally left. When Monday morning arrived I felt no different.

Chapter 11: Florida

BETWEEN THE TIME we arrived in Florida in 1999 and Tamma's death in 2007 we moved ten times to different rentals in various suburbs from West Palm Beach to Fort Lauderdale. With each move Tamma became more ill and our relationship more complicated. Her mental and physical decline tested my failing talent to repair her and finally distorted our relationship from one of mutual support and love to a dysfunctional codependent nightmare. The descent down the rabbit hole corresponded with a bizarre cast of characters, including minor and massive frauds and one suicide.

It started in Rhonda's brother's home. Our host, now completely obsessed with Tamma, spent his time complicating simple divorce and custody proceedings to insure maximum fees and devising new ways to impress Tamma. He had acquired his mysterious wealth when one of his clients bypassed his son and left his money to his own attorney, who happened to be Steven. Clearly this would be immediately suspicious but Steven had arranged for another lawyer to write the appropriate new will for this sole, one-time transaction. The full story as to whether the healthy demise was legitimately intended or not was never related to me but I was certain I had figured out how the magic trick was or could be done.

Tamma's party time with Steven encouraged me to find a new residence as quickly as possible. Steven was not happy when we moved to the nearby suburb of Lake Worth into a single family house on a small, man-made lake at least 20 minutes from his home. The house included, no extra charge, a paddle boat useful for quiet contemplation in the middle of the night with a glass of wine, or for Tamma a glass of vodka and a joint. During the daylight hours several ferocious red ant hills were an unwanted add-on.

This was a great house for a young married couple with two kids in strollers and a dog, but isolated and boring for a guy with an office

122

10 traffic-filled miles away in Boca and a wife who only wanted to party with Steven, who was now 8 potential DUI miles away.

We did manage to make friends with a transvestite and his significant other who lived a few houses away. This was not a lasting source of evening fun. When a bird managed to get in the house after about six months, clearly an evil omen, I decided to look for other housing, and with another two-month notice we were gone again.

I managed to answer an ad for a rental at a condo in Delray Beach called the Delray Beach Harbor Club. The two story units were quite dramatic and overlooked the attached boat club, which also offered a swimming pool. Tamma was not a swimmer but she could park herself on the pool deck and soak up the sun while I rode my new bike a few miles to my office. Our new landlord had made a fortune selling junk on cable TV infomercials and was very fair with the rent.

I raised the money for our new venture called June Fourth while I was still in Cleveland. The largest Cleveland investor quite reasonably insisted, since David was the key man, that we purchase insurance on David's life. We purchased a $ 1 million dollar term life policy on David and since the premium was so reasonable, at the same time, David decided to buy another $2 million dollar policy on his life for the benefit of his wife and two children not yet of college age. As additional backup, I asked Lenny (who had now moved permanently to Florida) to invest in the new venture. He assured me he would. And based on his assurance and support I had felt comfortable making the move. David's relationship with Lenny was complicated. As Concord had morphed into something different and basically downsized, David was not included in their future plans and was bought out.

Lenny backed out of his offer to invest almost the first week I landed in Florida. I was now two months into June Fouth and began to understand why. David's concept was clever but not properly tested. I had been under the assumption that he was "cash flowing" already and that his program, which involved a novel way for banks to earn CRA credits, was warmly received. The Community Reinvestment Act was designed to force banks to acknowledge their low income clients. Banks being bank-like did everything they could to avoid this new requirement. Basically David had a clever way for the banks to earn the credits without doing what they were supposed to do, make loans to low income people. All they would have to do was flip loans. Originate the loan and then immediately sell it. Earn the credit but not the risk. David was ahead of the curve. A few banks that David had a personal relationship were receptive but that was it.

David had a former Concord associate working for him when I arrived, who was under the impression that he had an option to purchase 25% of the new company at a meager price per share, balancing his non-existent salary. This was not my understanding or that of my investors. I confronted David and advised the employee it wasn't going to happen. He immediately walked out with the middle finger held high for both of us.

It became clear that June Fourth was going to be a rescue effort almost from the inception and that against my game plan for Florida, I was going to have to perform the rescue. My immediate solution was to enter the crazy world of subprime mortgages. Similar to David's world but different since it had a retail component.

David's office, which was now our office, looked more like a living room than an office. There were a few desks and lots of books and couches. An adjacent room, which he had rented for expansion (a crazy concept for an early stage company), had more traditional cubby hole offices that were for the time vacant. It was in the expansion room that we ran a retail subprime mortgage business.

David had more stories to tell than anyone I had ever met, except my grandfather. He was clearly very bright but there was a not so subtle bullshit about his rap. He said he graduated from Yale but I was pretty sure it was a Yale summer three week course, not the actual degree. Knowing David, that might have also have been an exaggeration. Possibly he just walked around the Yale campus one day, or like my brother's approach, read about Yale in a book. I knew a lot of lawyers who went to Harvard for three weeks in the summer for a continuing education class who put Harvard Law in their advertising material. David also confided in me that his dad had been an Air Force pilot, a war hero killed during WWII. This also proved not to be true.

I didn't socialize with David but knew he was into all the bullshit Palm Beach society happenings. His wife went to the proper church and very few people knew David was Jewish.

Tamma was accompanying Steven during many of his court appearances and being paid as moral support or for organizing his case file, anything he could think of to keep her around. I was actually beginning to welcome his attention because holding David's hand and rescuing a company seemed task enough. And Tamma was drinking more and sleeping less. And then to make matters worse, along came Bob.

I met Bob's wife Janet before I met Bob swimming in our condo pool with her son. A cute little boy in the water told me with some conviction that he could beat me in a swimming race. I said sure let's go at it and watched him paddle to the other side. After I congratulated him on his win, his mother introduced herself. She was a very Boca West New York Jew, but nice. Eventually she introduced me to her husband, Bob, who had been working on his boat which was docked in our harbor.

I expected Tamma home within the hour and so invited them all to dinner. We'd pick up some Chinese food and get acquainted. Their boat at the Harbor Club accounted for their pool use. Janet had told me they were in a business that had something to do with high end sunglass cases.

Bob looked like most of the better looking Italian guys that hung around little Italy in almost any Italian section of any large city. He had a nice giggle to his laugh and was very friendly. And I was soon to learn he was a world class alcoholic.

Back at the office I hired someone from Cleveland who was already in the subprime mortgage business, and we began to market the ridiculous loans we all now know about. I also tried to buy Cash Back Mortgage in Cleveland but realized they had too much debt and I would not be able to properly manage the business long distance. But we were up and running and had leased out some of the unused office space to a small broker dealer to help with expenses.

David was building a new house in West Palm Beach and had sold his Palm Beach Residence to pay for it. While it was being constructed David and the family had moved into an apartment building in Palm Beach. David never showed me the plans for the new house but he bragged about the several hundred volume library his office would include. I never counted David's money but assumed he was spending at the old Concord rate, which he could no longer afford.

While I was struggling at work Tamma had gone doctor shopping for a psychiatrist that would keep her well stocked in her favorite drug: klonopin. a prescription sedative useful as an anti-anxiety and anticonvulsant drug. Doctors prescribe klonopin to control or prevent seizures and reduce anxiety from panic attacks. Also known as clonazepam, this drug is a benzodiazepine—a class of drugs that is highly addictive. Tamma was now eating them like candy. Her first question to any doctor she called was: "Do you write?" If they wouldn't immediately prescribe her klonopin they were off her list.

Her new buddy Bob was hanging around his boat more often and Tamma was often hanging with him. I was not jealous but rather relieved that she seemed happier to have a buddy. I had gone with Tamma to a happy hour where the three of us were to meet up. When we arrived Bob was drunk at the bar with his head down, half off the bar stool. The manager was happy to see us and for us to remove the body. We took him back to the boat and called his wife to drag him home.

Bob was extending his drinking to later in the day and I was beginning to hear from the lady that controlled our gate to the complex that Bob and Tamma were beginning to attract the unfavorable attention of the management board of the condo association. My landlord was also at odds with the condo association so he never passed this news to me, but I was beginning to become disgusted with both their behaviors even without this additional information.

When Tamma was drinking she was actually civil; when Bob got drunk he became belligerent. We were at home one night when our friend the gatekeeper called us to say that Bob was at the gate. She would not let him in because he was drunk. His response was to scream at her, and she said she watched him make a wild U turn into the shopping center and that she hadn't seen him leave the car. He was probably still in his car.

Tamma and I went looking for him. When Bob saw me he jumped out of the car and started running. When I caught up to him I tried to get him into our car and drive him home. His reaction was to take a swing at me. I had had enough of his crap and grabbed him. I told Tamma to pop the trunk. I don't think she knew what I had in mind but she popped it. I picked up Bob and threw him in the trunk, shut the lid, and told Tamma to call his wife. We'd drive him home in the trunk. She begged me to come up with an alternative. I said, "fine," and drove him to a crappy motel about three miles away near the ocean. I rented a room for him for the night and then opened the trunk by his room door. He was passed out. I picked him up, carried him to the room, dropped him on the bed, and left the room key on the nightstand. The motel, we noticed a few years later, was the same hotel where the 9/11 bombers had lived while they learned how to fly but not land.

As Tamma's drug use and alcohol consumption were beginning to absorb her everyday life and spiral out of control, I hoped that a visit from her oldest friend and mother surrogate could bring her back to reality. That visit did not go well. Tamma was not interested in doing anything other than hanging out with a cocktail. Her friend gave up on her and went back to Cleveland.

127

When it became clear that the condo board had also had enough of her, my landlord said forget the rest of the lease.

"Wouldn't it be best if you move out now?"

So I found still another townhouse to rent, this time in West Boca. I moved all our stuff with the help of a couple of Jamaican movers, while Tamma remained drunk on the floor at the condo at the Delray Harbor Club. Disgusted, I told her to just stay there if she wanted to and left her in the now empty apartment. A day later, without explanation of where she had been, she moved in with me. We arranged separate bedrooms. I was finally done (I thought) and I gave her an ultimatum. Get some help. Start with a real psychiatrist. I think now that might be an oxymoron.

Meanwhile my dad was well into the first phase of Alzheimer's. Things were different back then. There was no such thing as Memory Care or day care. Dad was home and slept with mom. As things progressed we eventually had help during the day. Getting to understand what was happening to dad and mom's reaction was a learning experience. Sometimes there was associated humor.

Visiting mom and dad was a great break from the confusing life I was living in Boca Raton. My parents lived in Weston, Florida on the alligator alley. Next stop west was Naples. When the kids were young there were actually alligators on the golf course.

My mom, dad and I were all having dinner in our favorite little Italian restaurant, walking distance from the condo if you weren't in your 80's with Alzheimer's. Engaged in a lengthy conversation with my mother about nothing special I noticed that dad was no longer sitting with us.

"Mom, where's dad?"

"He went to the bathroom."

"Wasn't that a long time ago?"

"You might be right. You better go check on him."

I found him inside one of the two stalls in the bathroom.

"Are you alright?"

No answer.

I opened the door to find my dad panicked. His yellow sport coat was fine, hung neatly on the side of the door but his green pants were no longer green. My dad was a mess.

"Dad don't move. Just stay here I'll be right back."

I told mom about dad's embarrassing condition and suggested I needed to go home to get him some clean clothes. She said, "There's not time for that. There's a raincoat in the car." I got the raincoat and grabbed the garbage bag out of the trash receptacle in the bathroom and stripped dad. He didn't resist. I cleaned him up as best I could. His socks had to come off as well. I helped him put his shoes on, and then the raincoat. I grabbed his sport coat and watched the 83 year old beautiful man walk smiling out of the restaurant to the car. My mom pretended like nothing happened and never mentioned it again and no one noticed the naked man in the raincoat with tie shoes and no socks.

I think mom was prepared for the worst having watched her son, my brother, die in her condo. You never survive completely the death of your child.

Larry had been living in Cleveland and working but became too sick for a full time job. When his marriage ended he moved to Williamson and got a job running the technical part of Williamson's sole radio station. How my brother knew how to operate and maintain that equipment was a mystery to me. When my dad bought his sisters out of the clothing store, Larry gave up the radio gig and managed it. After the flood my dad had Larry supervise the reconstruction of the Schwachter Building. It was during this time that I finally had a chance

129

to enjoy my brother's unique perspective on life as his friend instead of his little brother. We both complained about our dad. My brother for being blamed about the day to day over the building transformation and my frustration with losing my money on what was a stupid plan from the inception.

After the building snafu was over and the building sold, my brother became very ill and came to Florida to seek better doctors. The news was not good. Larry had cancer, which spread quickly. He stayed with my parents in hospice until he died. Before that, Larry had driven up to Cleveland to visit old friends and stayed with me. I was unaware of how far his cancer had progressed and regret I was not at his side in Florida when he died.

Months after Larry died we discovered that he had a life insurance policy. The beneficiary was his divorced former wife, Kathy. Kathy wanted the money even though the beneficiary clause said "my wife Kathy" and she was not his wife and had not been his wife for many years. I was particularly angry because I had paid for my brother's divorce and the "one time" settlement to Kathy. We could not settle our dispute amicably, as in "lets split the money", so I went to court and argued that divorce terminated any rights she had. It was getting expensive for Kathy so she finally settled. The law is now changed in Ohio. Her claim today would not be valid.

Larry's illness was my father's chance pre Alzheimer's to make amends with Larry. I can't imagine what his death did to my mother. She never talked about it.

Soon my life in Florida would get even more confusing. David had a day marked on his calendar when his new house would be completed and he would finally close. The money held in escrow from the sale of his first house would be transferred to the escrow agent to accomplish the closing.

Things at June Fourth had become more critical. David could not meet payroll and I had already taken on some legal work to prepare for the end once it failed. David had assured me, though, that June Fourth would be rescued by a sale. He was negotiating with several buyers. One of the buyers was Frank Speight, who would be a principal player in my adventures in the future.

As the days passed I began to press David for more details on how potential sales were progressing. One day we went to lunch together to discuss more details and David drove so recklessly that I made him pull over. He let me drive back to the office.

One week later, I arrived at the office and found a manila folder on my desk with a handwritten note. "Here is information about your investor to move forward." Inside was the life insurance policy on David's life. The night before David had walked to a park bench near his temporary apartment and stuck a small caliber pistol in his mouth and pulled the trigger. David followed the same path as his father, who I would learn had not died during the war but had instead taken his own life.

After condolences and further investigation I learned that the policy on my desk had lapsed two months prior. Conveniently the policies he owned privately had not lapsed and had been paid for with June Fourth money. I'll never know if this was David's way of saying "F you" or if it was an honest mistake.

Fortunately David's wife's attorney was from one of the very best old line Palm Beach firms. He understood the potential for the damage a prolonged lawsuit would have on his client and agreed to a reasonable settlement. The settlement allowed me to pay off the creditors and restore the investors' funds, including my stock value and a fee for my efforts.

David's wife asked me if Lenny would loan her some money until the insurance proceeds were paid. I said I would talk to him. I called Lenny and confirmed that the insurance proceeds would be forthcoming but he declined to loan her money and decided he couldn't make it to David's funeral. David's wife decided to have the funeral on a Jewish holiday. I attended and at her request spoke since she had nothing planned. She insisted on an open casket notwithstanding the bullet hole in his head. "Don't worry, Richard, he looks wonderful. It was a small caliber gun."

If that suicide didn't freak me out, Tamma swallowed a whole bottle of sleeping pills in what I thought was a real attempt. As I rushed her to the hospital, she said she was just pretending. I was not equipped for that type of humor. The hospital "Baker Acted" her and two days later I picked her up after she was released. She laughed at me and told me they could never keep her in a facility. She knew all the tricks and could always get out.

During the next month, I spent time wrapping up June 4th and Tamma and I actually had fun spending a little bit of the money I got as a fee at the close. I fooled myself into believing she had become the girl I married in Cleveland. I bought her a new BMW convertible and we played in South Beach and the Keys. I bought myself a motorcycle and we toured the beach. Her good behavior prompted me to decide to move closer to civilization and when our lease was up we moved again to another apartment complex in Boca. Tamma agreed to see the head of psychiatrics at the Boca Hospital. I was hopeful that this was a new beginning.

CHAPTER 12: BLEEDER

YOUR DRIVER'S LICENSE is considered in law a privilege that can be revoked by the state that granted it if you refuse to be tested when suspected of driving "not quite all there." It used to be called driving while intoxicated (DWI). Now it's driving under the influence (DUI) to cover all our new ways of altering our consciousness.

The laws are pretty much uniform in all the states. If stopped, and you agree to be tested (blow or blood test) and flunk the test, that's strong evidence that you have committed a crime, which can be punished in a number of ways that may include imprisonment but almost always a substantial increase in your insurance rates. If you've been drinking it's usually a better bet not to blow.

Tamma usually drove under the influence of something or other. If not illegal drugs or alcohol, then prescribed drugs that impair your ability to drive. She was also a very bad driver on her best day often driving a hot sports car with the top down. But she only received one DUI in her long career and never suffered an insurance rate increase. For this I am to blame. Tamma kept her Ohio license and the "points" earned for a DUI for reasons unknown never transferred to Ohio. All Florida wanted was their punishment and fine. They apparently didn't care about Ohio. My insurance rates were never increased.

I was at home wondering where the hell she was since she was only going to the drug store to buy something related to her nails. All she needed was polish and some kind of number something file. But over two hours had passed. For anyone else this would be cause for concern but for Tamma every turn of the aisle was another adventure that could delay her. She was always shamelessly late.

She could have called me on her cell phone or returned my calls to her cell phone but that would require her hearing the ring of the phone, which was usually swallowed underneath her seat along with diet soda cans and mystery tissues. So when she finally answered my fifth or sixth call I was relieved until she responded by saying: "I'm lost." This was a surprise since the Walgreen was less than three quarters of a mile from the house. She said she was near the car wash so I immediately knew where she was and started to tell her she was only a few blocks away. But then her only response was "Oh shit!" and then the cell phone relayed a "capture and arrest" scene as Tamma was pulled over.

I could hear the officer ask for her license and registration and her slurred response: "I don't know where the fuck it is." That was the signal to turn off the TV and throw on the jeans and drive over to the intersection where I suspected she was being stopped. Approximately eight minutes later my suspicions were confirmed as I watched her stand on the corner of the street with her hands behind her back tied with the new plastic restraints that have replaced handcuffs.

Seeing her on the corner in handcuffs was not the shock for me it would have been for a normal husband. It was just another adventure in the world of aberrant behavior. So my response was not: "Hey, I'm an attorney. Let me speak to my client." It was instead:

"Officer, that's my wife. Can I speak to you for a moment?"

"Listen sir, he responds, "She's gone. You'll have to talk to her tomorrow. We can hold her 12 hours before we have to book her for DUI."

Now innocent, I forget the lawyer crap which I know won't work and respond:

"Oh no you misunderstand. I don't know anything about that. I just want to make sure she has her medicine."

"What do you mean?"

"Well, I'd like not to shout at you. Can you come a little closer? It's a bit embarrassing."

He approaches.

"Listen, you can take her in and have her blow that thing you use all day but she isn't drunk. She's just on some crazy prescription drugs. She isn't the best driver on a good day."

"What do you mean? If she's impaired SHE SHOULDN'T BE DRIVING."

"I cannot argue with that. I don't know if she's legally impaired. Her drugs are legally prescribed and she forgot them earlier and so if you are taking her in she MUST have them. I only live around the corner. Just please let me get them for her."

Tamma is now sitting down on the sidewalk looking like she couldn't care less and, in fact, is trying to scratch her nose with her shoulder with her arms behind her back and finding her failed attempts amusing.

The cop says: "What do you mean she MUST have them? What happens when she doesn't take her meds?"

"The truth, officer, which I didn't want to shout, is: SHE IS SEVERELY MENTALLY ILL and those drugs keep her from flying out of control."

He looks at her again, now even more involved in the nose scratch attempt.

"What exactly do you mean by flying out of control?"

"Well for openers" I say "she may try to bite you."

Now in my defense, I don't like to lie to the police, although they of course lie all the time, but actually she was a little nuts and didn't people do that kind of thing if they were crazy enough? So I exaggerated a little.

The officer who I was talking to was obviously the older senior guy and he shouted to his younger partner. "Henry; Cut her loose."

135

"Alright", he began, "here's the deal. Get her out of here. Take her home. And then get her car out of here within the hour. If I see her in the car in the next 12 hours she goes to jail, meds or not."

And so Tamma gets in the car and looks at me and says:

"Walgreens didn't have the fucking right nail files. Can you take me to CVS?"

A powerful hurricane swept from the east coast to the west and our power went out and stayed out. We had a friend in South Beach whose girlfriend was traveling out of the country. He said we could stay in her apartment for at least two weeks while she traveled. The power was not affected in South Beach and so we took advantage of the offer. Tamma seemed more relaxed and happier than I had seen her since we moved to Florida. But it was clear to me that she was now a full-fledged alcoholic. In my confused balance of evils I considered alcohol a welcome departure from drug use. And it certainly was cheaper.

When we returned to Boca her doctor suggested that Tamma go to the hospital for rehab, but she was resistant and refused. She had now been formally diagnosed with "bipolar affective disorder, mixed type". In the doc's words: "She has wide mood swings ranging from severe depression to severe excitement and elation." He added that there was a strong genetic component to this disorder. Tamma's mother and grandmother had both been schizophrenic. Tamma was inching in that direction.

Once her behavior was described in medical terms, for some reason I became less affected with displeasure by her worst behaviors. Knowing a physical condition was the catalyst for her bad behavior transferred my response from reprimanding a bad child to encouraging an adult to follow her doctor's advice. This new formal diagnosis fed into my codependent tendencies. It excused my insufferable desire to shield and parent her.

I was financially secure for now, many months ahead of the game, and so directed more attention to Tamma and "caring for her." So when she smashed her new car in the first of many fender benders, instead of anger there was "understanding." I was excusing things that needed not to be excused. And when I finally felt she was on a more even track, I went back to work. Accommodating bad behavior in the business world instead of at home, behavior I should have run from. My ability to overlook obvious character flaws made me an attractive target for business pros specializing in bad behavior.

Two bad characters had approached me while I was working at June Fourth and now sought me out again. They knew that I did private placements and was sometimes capable of raising equity funds. The first character had an airplane parts business where he was able to buy surplus parts from inventories no longer needed at large companies and then remarket them on the internet. This was actually a very good business. I did legal work for him and helped him raise a little money. Somehow, although his business was active and growing, he was funneling the profits into another entity and showing little gains or actual losses. In other words, he was a crook. When I discovered what he was doing, I went after him and he filed bankruptcy. He had an excellent attorney he obviously had used many times before and beat the rap. They were serial experts at screwing investors.

My next disaster association was with a nice Jewish guy from Jersey who said once too often

"To be perfectly honest…..."

If you have to say "to be perfectly honest" you probably are not. This was another potentially good business involving rural health clinics that would have been very successful if my Jewish guy was not a crook. The details are irrelevant.

But if these failed starts deterred me from ever finding the right people to work, with something changed with people David had introduced to me. David knew a father son real estate business in

Detroit specializing in buying properties leased to the federal government. They were looking for a guy with my credentials. They needed an attorney who had a Series 7 license who knew real estate to sit on their board in anticipation of forming a private REIT.

That private REIT was to grow into Government Properties Trust and be listed on the New York Stock Exchange.

While I was working for this new venture Tamma continued her drinking. I believed mental illness was actually mostly a physical disease and that Tamma's only cure would be a magic pill not yet developed. This was not a popular view in the United States, originating with early influences like Jonathan Edwards who preached about "sinners before an angry God." We have a long tradition of believing that all behavior off the norm is a result of sin or at the least failed discipline. My brain was tossed between two approaches. Hold out for science or lock her up somewhere.

The first time it happened she almost bled-out. It was terrifying.

Serious liver diseases such as cirrhosis can cause a number of complications, including esophageal varices: abnormally enlarged veins in the lower part of the esophagus, the tube that connects your throat and stomach. Esophageal varices develop when normal blood flow to the liver is blocked. The blood then backs up into smaller, more fragile blood vessels in the esophagus, and sometimes in the stomach or rectum, causing the vessels to swell.

Esophageal varices don't produce symptoms unless they rupture and bleed. Esophageal bleeding can be fatal.

Normally, blood from your intestine, spleen and pancreas enters your liver through a large blood vessel called the portal vein. But if scar tissue blocks circulation through the liver, the blood backs up, leading to increased pressure within the portal vein (portal hypertension). This forces blood into smaller veins in your esophagus, stomach and occasionally your rectum. The excess blood causes these fragile, thin-walled veins to balloon outward and sometimes to rupture and bleed. Once varices develop, they continue to grow larger.

To stop bleeding, the doctor uses an endoscope to snare the varices with an elastic band, which essentially "strangles" the veins, or a shunt where a small tube is placed between the portal vein and the hepatic vein, which carries blood from the liver back to your heart. The tube is kept open with a metal stent. The shunt is used when all other treatments have failed or as a temporary measure in people awaiting a liver transplant.

Doctor Cohen the gastroenterologist would use an endoscope to tie and bind her varices.

I had heard her vomit and then yell at about 3 am. She was in the bathroom and I could see a toilet bowl full of blood.

"I'm okay." She says.

"I'm not going to the emergency room. I promise if I bleed again I'll go to the hospital in the morning. Go back to bed."

Minutes later, it happens again. This time she does not make it to the bathroom and does the exorcist thing on the floor. I pick her up and throw her in the car and speed to the hospital emergency room. The waiting room is packed, and I am now screaming "Bleeder!" Where did I hear this, a TV rerun of ER?

She is immediately wheeled away from the stunned waiting room while I sign papers and answer legal questions as to whether or not I am empowered in various ways and of course whether or not the hospital has any hope of payment.

Once in the small internal waiting room Tamma vomits blood into the sink in huge globs of red congealed matter. In my shock I use my hand to force these unwanted discharges down the sink hole. Not a wise move for the health of the community. Now all Tamma wants is water and a clonazepam, two things she definitely cannot have. I discover from her confession that she swallowed four pills before she was admitted to calm herself.

The hospital resident who visits us first has attitude. He has branded her one more drug infected alcoholic who has ruined herself and he treats her accordingly. Maybe that was the truth but you want more for your loved ones and expect more from the hired help. And then since Tamma has uttered obscenities at a decibel level that could disturb even Zen like nurses, she is suddenly visited by Dr. Harvey Cohen, chief gastroenterologist of the hospital who essentially breaks it all down for the happy couple he is seeing for the first time.

She needs surgery (the endoscope procedure) which he would normally do immediately but he needs a little more history on her, so she will remain in the hospital overnight with, of course, no water (so he can do the tests he needs) and no fun drugs.

Tamma can live without food or drink for several days but not without drugs or alcohol which (without another entire long narrative description) ultimately results in her being physically restrained and "Baker Acted" once again by her psychiatrist also on the staff of the hospital. She is to be treated against her will.

She does get scoped, banded up and ultimately sent home after much screaming, mostly at me for being such a wimp. A follow up is scheduled for four months later.

The first time I saw Tamma take another drink, I moved out.

Tamma really didn't protest.

Even a sick codependent had his limits.

I found another rental a few blocks from the beach in Delray.

I left Tamma alone in the apartment after calling her family for help. None was forthcoming so I prayed that Tamma would sort things out on her own. The new place I rented had a great kitchen and, of course in the back of my mind, I was thinking Tamma would

140

love this place and maybe start cooking again. When I rented I told the landlord my wife was very sick in the hospital and I wasn't sure when she would be joining me so she would not be signing the lease.

I had a few trips to Detroit and a lot of roller skating on the streets near the beach, Steven visited with his new girlfriend, and then eventually Tamma moved in. Hopefully more self-aware. She was sober or at least not drunk. Her drinking had slowed way down.

There was a gay bar a block away that captured her afternoons on more than one occasion. I actually loved their cocktail hour and the piano player who took us back to the 40's. I think what was missing in her booze repertoire was now replaced with cocaine. I wasn't buying it for her. Probably her attorney friend, Rhonda's brother, was getting it for her. He visited the same bar. Although she had not worked for years, Tamma managed to have her own credit card with a large limit. She would always manage to get me to pay the minimum. When I stopped paying somehow she found the money for the minimum. Probably a cash advance from another credit card. She was good at the game.

Our new landlord hated Tamma and not necessarily for her behavior. She insisted on his actually doing the things landlords are supposed to do, and after our one year he was not willing to renew our lease and so off we went one mile away to the edge of Delray in a gated community and another two story townhouse.

Our new landlord, an attorney, called our old landlord for references and heard a torrent of expletives about Tamma, but he ignored the comments. He was impressed with my REIT story, fancied himself a real estate entrepreneur and rented to us anyway.

Tamma stayed home most of the time and seemed to become more depressed. She started drinking again. Now she was drinking the liquor chain's ABC house brand of vodka with lots of cranberry juice. I heard about a rehab place in Delray that was supposedly one of the best in the country. The downside was that it was very expensive and did not take insurance.

I decided to visit the place anyway since I could almost walk there. I found the place oddly in the "crackhead" part of Delray. Its front door was locked. Apparently the staff was on a break or in a conference or maybe it was just lunch time.

I sat outside on a bench near the door and watched a woman walk towards me lighting a cigarette from the end of the old one. She looked like she had been up all night. I assumed she was a patient. She sat on the bench near me and breathed out a half yawn and sigh. I said hello and asked her if she was a patient.

"Nope I just work here."

I told her I was hoping to check it out.

We exchanged the normal pleasantries and then she asked me if I was thinking about rehab for myself. I said no and then told her about Tamma and that I was just hoping to get some advice or ideas.

"There is no way I could afford this place."

We talked about the whole cycle I had been through with Tamma and about her diagnosis, her doctor, all of it. She seemed genuinely interested in my story. I got up to leave and thanked her for the talk. Only then did she tell me that she was the boss, the administrator.

"Go get your wife right now and let's see if we can get her some help. Don't worry about the cost. I'll try and sneak her through the cracks for a while."

I literally ran home to find Tamma asleep in bed.

I woke her up.

"Tamma, you can't keep doing this to yourself. You are going to die."

I told her about the place.

"Do you want to finally get some help? Please, you have to go right now."

She sat up and made direct eye contact and said. "Okay, I'll go."

"Just throw on some jeans, I'll get what you need later. We have to go right now."

Tamma seemed to know of the place and didn't put up an argument in the car. My friend remained in her office at the facility but I could see her at her desk and she gave me a little nod of acknowledgement when I walked in with Tamma. The intake process began immediately but did not go well.

Knowing Tamma, she probably managed to eat at least three clonazepam's before getting in the car. That should have kept her calm, but when the intake person told Tamma the basics, her first response was I am not giving up my meds. I need them.

"Tamma, we will give you something to stabilize you tonight but we need you clean for 24 hours before we can start recovery."

"Well that doesn't work for me. Call my psychiatrist. He's the head of the department at the Delray Hospital. I'm not giving up anything until he's involved."

"Of course we will be happy to get his input tomorrow but for now we need all your meds so we can evaluate you."

"I get it. I'm out of here."

Tamma walked out and headed for the car. My friend who heard it all now had her arm around my shoulder and just said, "She's not ready."

The following week we had a follow up appointment with her gastro doc, who confirmed that her liver was badly damaged and that if she didn't stop drinking she would be dead. He didn't say how long it would take to completely destroy her liver.

I attended Tamma's psychiatrist appointment a few days later and left in disgust. He was more afraid of Tamma than I was.

Meanwhile her mom was coming to visit and I hoped maybe she could take Tamma home with her and the combination of family and friends might help.

What happened instead was Tamma's mother found her lounge chair in my living room and waited to be waited on. Each morning during her two week stay she screamed at her daughter to take her to get her methadone. Each morning Tamma would refuse and I would transport her mother to the methadone clinic and wait in line for her until it was almost her turn. I actually didn't mind the wait since I met the regulars. I was surprised to see so many high school kids who had become hooked on prescription drugs. Methadone is no picnic. It's a narcotic without the high and a money maker for the state. Ironically you have to withdraw from methadone as well.

So mom's main gift was 10 or 12 more holes in the carpet and more ashtrays to empty.

After she left, Tamma's sister and brother-in-law's showed up as enforcers to get money from Tamma they said she owed for drugs. They threatened me with a baseball bat but were too high to properly swing it. I was not seriously frightened, just disgusted.

We had once again worn out our welcome with our latest landlord. He did not take kindly to the destroyed carpet and extensive cigarette smoke. Our deposit would not cover the carpet and painting. He was an attorney and didn't need to hire one so he sued me for free to recover the more extensive damage. I decided to settle after he overwhelmed my time with interrogatories and legal annoyances.

I dragged Tamma to our last apartment together in Delray Beach.

CHAPTER 13: WEST PALM BEACH

I rented our last townhouse where we would live together in Delray Beach. Once again I did this without Tamma's knowledge. Her name did not appear on the lease and as far as the complex knew she didn't exist. It was "don't ask and I won't tell you that my wife is an alcoholic occasionally visited by a crack dealer." By now I had stopped trying to deter Tamma from doing anything damaging to her body. If she wanted alcohol I would get it for her. Whatever else she did was beyond my pay grade. If I didn't get her alcohol she'd get it herself and risk another DUI or worse, an accident involving another car and or injury to someone innocent. And apparently her crack dealer delivered.

Tamma belonged in an institution. She was drinking more. I found a crack pipe I suspected was hers or one of her friends. She was showing signs of severe liver damage. If you gripped her arm too hard it would become black and blue. She had called the police more than once telling them I had beat her up. Of course, this was ridiculous and the police after they arrived saw the obvious, but she was black and blue and at least once they suggested I leave, at least for the night. I said I would but I just drove to the drug store a block away and when I returned she was asleep for the evening.

Our friend Eddie who we visited often in Naples, was also an alcoholic and had damaged his liver. His eyes and skin were showing the signs, the yellow tint, the buildup of bilirubin, the billboard for jaundice, liver failure and ultimately death. Tamma saw this and knew the risks for herself but was not deterred.

Fortunately work kept me sane. My small Detroit federal government property private REIT had now grown to public company status on the New York Stock exchange. This evolutionary process kept me very occupied and energized by the new experience and opportunity to be "among the living." We had quarterly board meetings in Omaha and I had a daily "sourcing efforts" job looking for potential acquisitions. The board members were all interesting accomplished guys. One of them became my angel.

Our first introductory meeting of the new board members occurred at an old famous Italian restaurant in Palm Beach, Florida.

I have the "on time "disease and usually arrive early for every appointment. Frankly I was also nervous. I had spent too many hours alone with Tamma and wasn't really sure my actual sane voice worked. By now the dialogue in my head was so advanced that although I was not audible I was frequently talking to myself. If I wasn't sitting alone in my office, I was wandering the beach or riding my motorcycle alone with my thoughts.

There was a bar adjacent to the restaurant's dining room and I considered a calming drink before the rest of the new board members arrived. There was no one in the bar except one well-dressed man alone at a table for two in the corner of the bar. He had a drink and I did not. So I asked him if there was a bartender working the room. "I'm very early for a meeting and I need a drink."

"I am as well. Come join me, he's actually on an errand for me. I requested a special bottle of scotch for my meeting."

His name was Spencer and yes, he was one of the new board members, also punctual. I would learn he was a brilliant attorney with a Wharton MBA and a law degree from Villanova. He was also the underwriter's control representative. His job was to make sure on behalf of the guys raising the money that the board knew what they were doing.

Spenser championed me. He knew I was the only one on the board who had actually owned and operated real estate. When he learned from my homework that our pool of potential acquisitions was much smaller than had been represented, he insisted that I also

146

become involved with the day to day sourcing of properties. Although there were free standing GSA (Government Service Administration) properties, many of the government offices were in larger buildings with other tenants who were not GSA. Could we buy these buildings and still be true to our stated mission? The question was for me to figure out. The other board members were not happy with this arrangement but Spencer prevailed.

Spencer proved to be my first experience with an adult who actually was interested in helping me with no other agenda. I knew little about his personal life other than he was buying his dream home in Florida and had some health issues. He had survived Hodgkin's as a younger man, a fact I was to learn much later.

The board had a Fourth of July party in Omaha, and as always I debated whether to take my wife. Would she self-destroy during the evening and embarrass herself and me. I weighed the risks and decided a trip anywhere would be good for her and she actually seemed excited to go. Ironically most of the board and wives were more inebriated than she. Tamma was on her best behavior but I did see her drift away to talk to one of the bartenders and by the end of the evening she appeared, at least to me, to be high on cocaine. Clearly none of the

147

board noticed and I was glad to safely fly home at the end of the weekend without the need for explanations. Spencer knew my story and was always ready to listen. He was one of the few.

It was getting more difficult to live in the same apartment with Tamma. The kitchen on the first floor remained Spartan, well organized and spotless while the upstairs was a disaster. The disarray in Tamma's mind had not transferred to the one place still sacred to her. She drank and did drugs but strangely followed the Michael Pollan rules and ate "real food, not too much, mostly plants." She would eat steamed vegetables and drink herbal tea because "eating right was the thing to do."

Tamma was rarely dressing now or leaving the house. She'd wear her K mart robe and slippers that a child would wear with a little bear at the toes. She was naked under the robe with her skinny legs exposed and black and blue marks everywhere. As if her liver were screaming: "Notice me, I'm dying!"

When I told her I needed to move out she was perched on one leg with the other foot firmly on her other thigh making a cup of tea.

"I don't know why you have to move out and pay two rents. You know you'll never divorce me. And besides, if you leave me who will have a girl such as myself?"

I respond:

"Someone with lots of money who likes to do drugs."

"And you never did drugs when you were my age? What a hypocrite. Cocaine, pot, Quaaludes. You did it all."

I no longer wanted to battle back. I had given up on these contests. How could I continue to fight with someone who was in her bathrobe with a distended stomach, jaundiced eyes, a belly retaining fluids, and a failing liver.

The next week I took her to her four month follow up doctor appointment with Dr. Cohen. Somehow on this day, the reality of her physical condition overwhelmed me and I could not suppress my tears.

"What are you worried about, big boy?"

"If I die look at all the alimony you'll save. And besides remember how short my life line is. Remember the palm reading. This was never supposed to be a happy ending."

In the lobby I noticed all the patients I used to think were old at an age I would never have to reach. Getting old was something for others, not me. The geriatric army was in Cohen's waiting room. They pushed walkers and stared into space with vacant eyes. How old were they? They were supposed to die eventually, not a young woman not yet 46. Not Tamma. Not me.

Tamma signed in at Harvey's office and I told her I would wait in the hall. I really did not need to see the doctor. I would help her follow Harvey's instructions for rehab and cure but she was on her own. If she wanted to get better, she had to do this herself. This lie sounded good to me and I marched outside. Twenty minutes later I poked my head back into the lobby and didn't see Tamma. The receptionist said she was in with Harvey. I went back outside looking for a restroom. When I returned she was smoking a cigarette sitting on the ground outside his office in the open air hall.

"Well, I'm dead."

"What do you mean? No more drinking of course. Did he say no smoking either?"

"No he told me I only have six months at most to live."

"What!"

I went charging back into Cohen's office, ignored the receptionist and banged on Harvey's door.

"Did you tell her she has six months left to live?"

"I did", he says, "if she keeps drinking, which she obviously is doing."

"If she's living alone she will also probably bleed out in her sleep, too weak to call for help."

"Well what if she has a nurse and does everything she is supposed to? Then what is her prognosis?"

"Maybe a couple of years. Her liver is very damaged. I'm sorry."

Back out on the office deck where the smoker sits, apparently without an apparent care in the world, all I can muster is : "No, he did <u>not</u> say you would be dead in six months. Only if you keep drinking." I ignored the rest of the conversation with Harvey about the two years. I was sure she never entertained that polemic. Hell, I could be dead in two years, I rationalized. So I hugged her and drove her home with a promise of a nice dinner. Like no big deal.

Once alone, I finally accepted the obvious, that she would not stop drinking and could die. So beautiful, so young yet so damaged. If she were to die what would die within me, or would the converse occur? Would I reawaken from the dead?

Tamma was not my only concern. My father had followed the normal Alzheimer track and passed away. I had a deal with my mother that he could remain home as long as he didn't hit her. Once that happened she agreed he could no longer live there.

That day finally came. My mother tried to help him on with his socks and he struck her hard in the arm. I told her to call 911. She agreed but not until I arrived. I called and told the dispatcher the situation so they did not come with guns blazing. Actually they sent a young attractive policewoman, who my dad seemed to enjoy as she led him to the locked psych ward of the Broward County Hospital.

"Memory care" facilities did not exist and it would take two months of our visits to a mental ward where my dad sat locked in a highchair for adults before we could get a nursing home to admit him. He lasted in the nursing home exactly two days before he had a massive heart attack and was rushed to the closest hospital in Fort Lauderdale. My mom and I were with him moments before he died. Still looking handsome as ever.

The new problem was the hurricane, which had knocked down power lines and left my mother alone with only emergency power for the hallways but no power for the refrigerator or stove. Gas pumps didn't work at most of the gas stations. Without a generator to power the pumps the station was useless. Walmart had generators but also very long lines.

The trip to my mother's and back was over 60 miles so gas would be a problem. I had to go there every day to check up on her status. My enormous tip/bribe came to the rescue at Walmart and I was able to beat the line. I ran an extension cord to the light socket in the hallway of my mom's condo, where the generator kept the lights and elevator working. That saved the refrigerator and we played cards hoping things would power up. They didn't until two days later but I went back and forth until things returned to normal.

Both my kids had their own trauma during this time, but I will let them tell their own stories now that they are both grown men with their own children.

Sometimes when I visited my mother if Tamma was sober I would take her along. Tamma loved my mother and on her last visit to my mom asked my mother if she could move in with her. Tamma said she could cook for my mom and they would be great company for each other. My mom told Tamma if she would stop drinking she thought it would be a great idea.

Now that my heart was being shredded I sought succor from Al Anon. Tamma always used the excuse to avoid AA that she was Jewish and that their higher power was Jesus and "what's up with that." The only preaching she respected was Mothers Against Drunk Drivers.

"They're okay. They're not telling me to stop drinking, just not to drink and drive."

"I can support that."

My problem with Al Anon had nothing to do with the higher power business. I'd love to believe in God, I'm just waiting for evidence I can understand. What I couldn't handle was what I perceived as a total lack of empathy. As a true codependent the idea of distance was not something I could understand.

At my first and last meeting, was a mother there whose daughter was pregnant and out on the street. What she yearned for was some compassion. Maybe a group hug. What she got instead, at least as I perceived it, was a lecture. I couldn't endorse these tactics even if they were the right approach.

Spenser did not show up for our last June Fourth board meeting and I learned for the first time that he was ill. This surprised me since Spenser was always the first one in the gym in the morning at whatever hotel we were staying at. We would be on adjacent elliptical machines discussing the news or the day ahead.

I decided to visit Spenser at his new home in North Miami Beach and finally met his wife Carmen. I learned that his radiation cure for Hodgkin's disease had now caused lung cancer years later. Apparently this was always a risk. A few weeks later Spenser was in a hospital bed in his downstairs living room with a large screen TV turned to CNBC so he could monitor his holdings. I never read "Tuesdays with Morrie," but the following weeks until Spenser's death were Thursdays with Richard and Spenser. He never once talked about his illness. I would arrive at the house and say hello to Carmen and then kick her out the door. She needed to take a break but never would have asked for help.

After many weeks of visits I learned that Spenser was no longer at home but had been readmitted to the hospital. Carmen was sleeping in the room with him. I told admittance to ring the room to see if I could visit. I told them I was a relative.

Spenser was surprised and happy to see me. While I was visiting a rabbi came to visit with a sad look on his face to see if there was anything Spenser would like him to do. Spenser said no thank you and when the rabbi left started to laugh. I said my goodbyes. Spenser was taken home the next day for hospice at home. He died a few days later. After Spenser's death I got to know Carmen and understood how their marriage lasted almost 30 years. She had her own grace and warmth.

I couldn't work at home with Tamma and so went looking for an office to rent. I thought downtown West Palm Beach would be fun. During my search I stumbled on Frank Speight. The same Frank I had met a few years before with David Bernard.

Frank's office was in the Comeau Building on Clematis Street, the happening street in downtown West Palm. On the other side of the intercostal is snob city, Palm Beach where nothing much happens. Clematis street had the restaurants, bars and nightlife. His office caught my attention as I walked through the historic building.

His conference window opened to the arcade displaying a rendering of a hotel project to be constructed in Belize. Frank was in his office and I took the opportunity to become reacquainted. I told him I was busy with the REIT but looking for a place to hang out. My home office was boring. He had an extra office and said just come in whenever you want.

"No rent, it's not being used. Maybe we can do some things together." That first encounter would end a few years later with the following news report. You don't achieve the following notoriety without having a larger than life personality.

Chief Executive Officer of International Stock Transfer Pleads Guilty in $3 Million Securities Fraud Scheme

153

BROOKLYN, NY—*Yesterday, Cecil Franklin Speight, also known as Frank Speight, pleaded guilty to conspiracy to commit mail fraud and securities fraud for engaging in a conspiracy to steal over three million dollars from investors. Speight was the sole owner, officer, and director of International Stock Transfer (IST), a registered transfer agent with the United States Securities and Exchange Commission (SEC) since May 2004. According to court filings and facts presented at the plea hearing, Speight stole at least $3.3 million from victim investors and used the proceeds to pay personal expenses, including purchases at Mercedes Benz, Nordstrom, Netflix, and Groupon. Speight faces up to five years' imprisonment, at least $3.3 million in restitution, and a fine equal to double the investors' losses.*

The guilty plea was announced by Loretta E. Lynch, United States Attorney for the Eastern District of New York, and George Venizelos, Assistant Director-in-Charge, Federal Bureau of Investigation, New York Field Office (FBI).

"Rather than transferring capital to issuers, the defendant used the investors' funds as his own, including financing his lifestyle in Florida. His victims, from the Eastern District of New York and around the world, were conned into buying bogus securities that were not worth the paper they were printed on. Now, he will be held to account for his crimes," stated United States Attorney Lynch. Ms. Lynch extended her grateful appreciation to the Federal Bureau of Investigation, the agency responsible for leading the government's investigation, and thanked the Securities and Exchange Commission for its assistance.

"Speight tricked his victims into thinking their money would be invested in high-yield securities, but he was essentially using their investments to fund his own lifestyle to the tune of several million dollars. People have the right to trade in an uncorrupted market, and today's guilty plea is proof of the FBI's continued determination to root out those who unlawfully interfere with this process," stated FBI Assistant Director-in-Charge Venizelos.

IST was founded by Speight in 2004 as a transfer agent registered with the SEC with offices in Palm Beach, Florida. Speight used "cold callers" and other means to entice victims into investing their money in allegedly high yield securities. Speight promised the victims a high rate of return if they invested in securities that were purportedly associated with IST. Speight and his co-conspirators directed the victims to wire their investment funds into purportedly secure attorney escrow accounts. Once the victims wired money to those escrow accounts, Speight typically stole the funds for his personal use, including the purchase of a Mercedes Benz automobile. Speight also withdrew over $350,000 of investors' funds in cash.

Today's guilty plea took place before United States Magistrate Judge Roanne L. Mann at the federal courthouse in Brooklyn, N.Y.

The government's case is being prosecuted by Assistant United States Attorney Jack Dennehy.

Moving into Frank's office my only goal was to get out of the apartment. Tamma was getting worse and I could not sit home and watch her die. I talked to an attorney about a divorce. My concerns were the legal ramifications of her downhill slide. Tamma was spending faster than I could earn and beginning to be associated with some drug dealers. I couldn't jeopardize my board seat with even the least bit of suspicion of less than stellar behavior. Frequent police appearances at the door could not be tolerated by a board member of a New York Stock Exchange Company. I told Tamma my plans but she was convinced I would never leave her. I assured her even if we were divorced I would always take good care of her. I was already feeding her and doing her laundry. She barely got out of bed. I was prepared to see her through to the end just not as her husband. We weren't sleeping together and there was no physical intimacy between us. I wanted my own place for mental health. I think she believed me when I told her I would always take care of her.

After several months and several trips to Belize helping Frank with some of his new investors and projects, I decided to rent a condo from Frank that he had bought as an investment. The condo was in a new building in downtown West Palm, walking distance from the office.

I knew by then from our trips together that Frank was a bullshitter, but that didn't make him a criminal. I wasn't making any money with Frank but I liked the condo and its rent and loved the trips to Belize, which he paid for. The trips were like mini vacations from Tamma and my mother duty

155

Belize, formerly British Honduras, was an interesting contrast from Jamaica. It was three countries in one. You could visit the jungle and Mayan ruins, you could bank in a sophisticated Central American English speaking city where the citizens were educated and compassionate, or you could go to one of the Cayes and enjoy some of the finest diving in the world and ride around in golf carts with high end tourist attractions.

Frank's project was near the airport and made sense, and it might have been successful if he hadn't stolen all the investors' money and diverted it to his own elaborate lifestyle. By the time all of Frank's misdeeds were discovered, I was no longer living in his condo because my mother had died. Meanwhile Tamma was living out her remaining short life on the beach.

CHAPTER 14: JAYNE

AFTER MY DAD DIED my mom stayed active, played bridge and mahjong, went out to dinner with friends but eventually slowed down and no longer wanted to go anywhere. She needed some help with her "day to day," whether she wanted to admit it or not. Since I was the last one standing in my core family, I was the obvious and only choice to help. My mother and Tamma became my daycare juggling act.

Mom was no longer driving and seldom left the condo, spending most of her time with crosswords and television. I knew she was not herself when the night manager called me to report she appeared in the lobby in the middle of the night half naked. I started my part time caregiver job by handling her financial issues and her mail. To help with fiscal sanity, it was clear her Grand Marquis had to go.

My mother reminded me they bought the Grand Marquis because of its bench seats:

"Only the Lincoln and Ford have the big bench seat. That way your father and I could fit three couples comfortably in the car."

Clearly the dealership never mentioned that a burned out headlight for the car would cost $350 to replace, that the oversized beast averaged 12 miles a gallon and that its resale (salvage) value would never equal the unpaid associated secured debt. Although the car still drove level on the road, to the bank it was "upside down."

I was now driving to mom's condo in Weston at least twice a week. The condo was exactly 57 miles each way ($22 in gas). One "This American Life" podcast and one quarter "Fresh Air podcast" away. With traffic you could add a few of Bach's English Suites.

One of my first visits concerned the new microwave and oversized toaster oven I purchased to ease meal preparation for mom.

157

I was cooking a weeks worth of meals that only needed reheating. In between these meals mom could make her beloved chicken pot pies or one of Stouffers other offerings. The $400 microwave I had purchased had many options but if you just wanted to keep it simple only three buttons at the bottom of the controls, all in a row, needed to be activated. *Reset/Quick-Min/Start.*

"Mom, you push the first one to clear it. The second one for the cook time. Push it once for each minute. And then just push start."

"But what if I only need a ½ minute?"

"Just open the door early."

After a lot of practice, she actually got it. I put tape over all the other controls so she would go directly to clear/reset. But there was a new problem. She was not strong enough to activate the buttons. Ever enterprising, I bought a giant toaster oven that had a simple twist on knob that was also a timer that turned the toaster oven off, solving the problem and avoiding the actual full size oven which had almost burned the condo down when it remained on for 10 + hours.

The "I Love Lucy" show could have been shot in my mother's apartment. All that was missing was Fred and Ethel. The place was frozen in 1954. The walls were painted peach to better explore the color-TV phenomenon. The drop ceilings in the kitchen and bathrooms celebrated new plastic technology. The eclectic lamps were enormous. (You needed a crane to lift them). Her famous tchotchkes took two forms: those that were silver plated and those that were porcelain. The silver plated items would take an army of maids to polish properly. As to the pottery, if you have seen one "Balloon Lady" you have seen them all.

Jayne did reign on her throne. My mother at 91 still knew how to crack Dentyne gum and multi-task. The TV was on loud enough for the neighbors to enjoy and the "clicker" remote always stood ready. She wore her peignoir in the classic way (sans underwear) and rarely left the bed. Vanity on display, she made sure her shapely legs remained visible at all times. Wasn't Lucy a dancer before she met Ricky?

Mother in her Ruth Gordon style once began:

"I know you think I'm stupid."

"I don't."

"But I am. I can't remember how to work anything. The truth is I don't like food anymore except peanut butter."

"OK Mom, so my truth is I only like pizza and black coffee and I am not even sure coffee is food."

"But you can work a microwave."

"You can knit."

"I just feel awful that you have to come over here to feed me."

"STOP BEING SO NICE TO ME! I was a shitty mother."

"What are you talking about? He kisses her, "You were the hottest mom on our street. That counts too."

Next to her bed was a hands free phone I had bought her with an alarm that sounded like an Eisenhower "duck and cover" air raid with a flashing light built in. My mother refused a hearing aid.

"Go ahead and get me one if you must, but the second you walk out the door it will be out of my ear."

"Mom, get dressed and let's go get dinner, go to the grocery store and the drug store. And we need to talk about getting you a little more help."

"Okay, but I'm fine."

"Humor me, mother."

Her smile was not "full flash" anymore. Possibly because she had some teeth pulled and no longer liked her smile. To mom if it didn't look good it wasn't of value. More likely her smile left her because she was ill. In fact, she was in heart failure. But the doctor had said it was the good kind. Right side or left? I couldn't remember. Was there really a good kind?

For mom the heart problem was merely a wardrobe issue. She had a belly for the first non-pregnant time in her life and worst of all her ankles were swollen. Refusing to associate this with a heart issue she was now dieting as a solution. Pork ribs with lots of barbecue sauce were still on her diet (as was all Chinese food and pepperoni pizza.) And then there was the issue of the nasty sore on her arm she considered unsightly. So long sleeves were required, even if it was 83 outside.

"I can't understand why this thing won't heal."

"The doctor is lousy. I've been there three times and it just gets worse."

I knew that it didn't heal because it was not your everyday sore. At first I guessed the fair skin beauty had skin cancer. My guess was wrong. It was a "sea monster cancer" that had sought the surface for air. Probably she had lung cancer. But whatever the cancer's name, it had now metastasized and consequently the sore. I talked to the oncologist. After a review of all the options, the sensible plan was to do nothing. Enjoy the ribs. Stay happy.

I watched her walk down the hall for our lunch and shopping trip.

"These damn shoes stick. I can't find comfortable shoes. Nobody has my size 7.5 quad A. My arch is supreme."

So was her ramrod posture.

"Mom, why not wear tennis shoes like everyone else?"

"I'm not like everyone else. I will drive." She goes for the keys.

"You're too busy on the phone or playing with the CD player. I'm scared to death driving with you."

Like many seniors she can't remember her last accident but many anonymous drivers have certainly been witness to accidents her driving has caused.

"Mom, how did I possibly get here without your help?" He won't give the keys up.

"We're just going a few blocks. I'll drive. Besides your license has expired and you're uninsured, not that any of that would stop you."

"Fine, but go to Walgreens first. That's where my real business is."

When I walked with her the whole world slowed down. If I walked behind her she would stop and get distracted. If I walked ahead of her I was being rude. So it was kind of a buddy date walk into the drugstore directly to the cosmetics department. Why a woman 91 who rarely left her bed cared about anti-wrinkle cream was a mystery to me. But there we were considering product with adjectives like replenishing, restructuring, correction line repair, cellular, re-moisturizing, lift firming, all for only $150. And of course none of them would be effective even if she was much younger. She also wanted one with the most sun protection although she never left the house. Something called "FREEZE 24/7".

"Can we eat Mom? Please! I'm hungry and I have a long ride home."

Lunch at her favorite rib joint required parking temporarily in a wheel chair spot, without the proper credentials, getting Mom out of the car and walking her to the door and hoping to find a place for her

161

to sit while I parked the Beast. This had to be done quickly so I didn't get a ticket. Tamma once had decided if she parked her small foreign car in the space between two handicapped spaces that somehow that was okay and did not warrant a ticket. The $250 fine I paid for her was not a lessen to her but kept me ever diligent about respecting the few benefits afforded to the disabled.

After I watched her very slowly eat an entire slab of ribs but no salad or potato or drink a single sip of liquid she was ready to talk. She began:

"Okay, so what's up?" She smiles at me and bats her eyelashes just for fun.

"Are you getting married again? Did you knock someone up?"

"I should never have told you that sex was great."

"Mom, you're 91! I am embarrassed."

"So/"

"Did I ever tell you how gentle your father was with me? You know he was very big and I was very small."

"MOM...just stop now please! You need more help. We paid for home health care so please can we use it?"

"Sure. The last wonderful lady you had over for me probably stole the few valuable pieces of jewelry I still have."

"We can't prove that, mom. I thought you told me your ring just fell off."

"I can tell you anything I want! You were always a little gullible."

"Come on, you like Miss Jeannine. I am just going to ask her to come on the weekends now as well."

162

"Fine," she concedes. "She is my new black daughter."

On the way out of the restaurant I get appreciative stares from the older women. Such a good son!

Ironically the Sunday Jeannine began her first weekend mother duty, she found mom on the floor with her head wedged between the nightstand and the frame of the bed. She was breathing but not responsive. Her job began and ended with a 911 call.

It had been two weeks since she was rushed to the Westin Florida Cleveland Clinic. After the 911 call I had raced there, and found her silent and paralyzed on the left side. A few days later, she could talk but sounded like she'd had a few. She could still not move her left side. This seemed to my mother a mere inconvenience.

"Just get me home."

I knew that would not be possible. Even with home health care, she would need 24/7 attention. While I was pondering my lack of options a young Asian doctor entered. Curiously his name tag read "Dr. Samuel Cohen". Noticing my reaction the young doctor began:

"Yup, it's my name. Surprised?"

Stammering: " *Oh no. I guess….*"

"Yeah. Well it's worked well for me. "

"Now here's the deal; rehab needs to start immediately if she is to get her functioning back."

The doctor picks her up until she is standing next to him but supported by his arms and starts letting herself support her own weight.

"Ha. You are one hell of a dancer." slurs Mom.

"Okay. You're in good hands, mom, I've got to talk to someone. "Be right back." I left her with the doctor.

Racing to the front desk, I assumed that a hospital that has valet parking must have some kind of a patient ombudsman. Finding her on the next floor down I started:

"Help!" "My 91 year old mom is here with a stroke and I don't have a clue what happens next."

Her name tag red "Ms. Rodriguez".

Three months later, I would stand in this same room and argue with Annette, and my mother's doctor whether mom should be transferred to hospice. By then I would be on a first name basis with Ms. Rodriguez. But that first meeting proved to be a font of information. A proper rehab place was selected aka nursing home and all the financial rules were explained, including how I might cleverly qualify for Medicaid if Medicare coverage ran out. This was followed by my mother's transfer to a nursing home and then the inevitable return to the hospital. When my mom was in the nursing home, my respect for the caregivers was enormous. They took extra good care of mom knowing I would be visiting weekly. I took the time to learn their names and always thanked them.

When I got the call from the nursing home that she had taken "a turn for the worse," I asked that they take her back to the Cleveland Clinic as opposed to the hospital across the street. They humored me and agreed. The Cleveland Clinic staff only knew that her vitals were very bad and that she did not have too much longer. The operative word to me was what is "longer?" A day? A few hours?

She was in room 709 looking less regal. She felt warm to my hug and she spoke to me only with her eyes.

"Mom, do you know where you are?"

Almost a whisper responds: "Hospital!"

"Yes, but we will get you out of her soon as we can." I lied.

She seemed to be fading. Her skin was opaque, almost translucent.

164

Wasn't there a movie where the character started to fade if you ceased to believe? A children's story? I grabbed her again and said:

"I love you mom."

Was that enough to keep her alive?

Did she respond? I wasn't sure.

"I will be right back mom. I have to talk to someone."

That talk began:

"Look Annette, I don't care if they want the room or not, she is too sick to move to hospice. I'm not sure she will make it another night."

"Her doctor thinks so Let me get her." Annette has that very concerned professional look that probably was sincere.

The floor doctor appeared who was not discourteous but also not in the mood to counsel a 91 year old patient's son.

He echoes Annette:

"I'm sorry, it's time for hospice. We can't do much more now."

I respond: "You might be right but she is too sick to move. Come look at her."

As we entered 709 and I approached the bed, I knew that she died while I was briefly out of the room. The form in the bed was no longer my mother. Her eyes were fixed open looking empty or maybe at the heaven I now wished existed. I tried to close her eyes. They do not close. I stared at the empty form. A life size doll without a battery. I hoped her soul had flown into me where I could protect it and safely pass it to my children and grandchildren.

As she had wished, I cremated her. I placed the notice in the paper, said the appropriate prayers and then was alone with only memories.

My brother, mother and father were now all dead.

I was the last one standing.

My mother would outlive Tamma by eight months.

CHAPTER 15: POMPANO BEACH

Hey. Richie,

I know you are sick of these pathetic letters, so I'll make this one short and sweet.

You said Today you wanted to move back to Cleveland, I think you should—but I can't—I have been shunned by my family—let alone the fact I have NO FRIENDS THERE OR HERE.

You have been so wonderful to me. I am a drunken drug addict. I serve no purpose to anyone I am a waste of a human being. I could not even ~~keep~~ keep a friend that I only saw 2 or 3 times. The people on the computer were just tests.

Kevin kept telling me God will save me from myself. Why did God let Rhonda & Sheryl die—I pray every nite not to wake. These were 2 people who were loved and are missed by so many. I don't even have 10 people who aren't related to me that would show up at my funeral. It doesn't make sense to me. Is there any reason?—

The only person who has stayed in contact w/ me is a convict—I apologize for letting ~~Bob~~ make you so miserable. What made you think that you could ~~save~~ me? You washed me up and dressed me—but I'm still the same gutter trash—

1) Save Yourself - what you think is a pain, I envy - a family that loves me too much.

2) I want nothing — I will go to work —

3) You are entitled to a WIFE WHO FUNCTIONS - Not some slug who lays IN BED ALL DAY.

4) Get Rid OF THIS LOSER!! You ARE making yourself A VICTIM IF YOU choose to stay with ME!

5) I WILL NOT Kill Myself - I have TRIED - I'M NOT EVEN capable OF THAT - what a pathetic thing to admit to —

PLEASE BE HAPPY — MAKE A LIFE FOR YOU — BE SELFISH ; YOU deserve IT! YOU HAVE ALWAYS TRIED TO SAVE PEOPLE — YOU ARE No. 1 — HERSELF Society.

THANK YOU FOR PRETENDING TO CARE - LET ME GO — PLEASE! You stand to GAIN Nothing except disappointment AND MISERY — RUN —— How MUCH DO YOU WANT TO TAKE?? WHEN IS ENOUGH — I'm NOT FIXABLE, HAVEN'T YOU figured THAT OUT? MY OWN parents Don't CARE — Why do you?

TAMMA AND I HAD NOT BEEN LIVING TOGETHER for several months when the Delray apartment lease expired. The management of the apartment complex had been trying to reach me. There was now a large dent in our attached garage and they wanted to confirm that I was the culprit and inquire about my insurance. Tamma of course professed ignorance although there did appear to be a new dent in her BMW. Since the management was unaware of her existence, these discussions became even more

168

awkward. As far as they were concerned the BMW was my car, my responsibility. Fortunately insurance would cover the damage.

The move out date was not a surprise to Tamma. We had discussed it at length as well as her future plans for living separately in her own place. She wanted to live on the beach in a furnished place. She had her heart set on a converted motel in Pompano Beach. I thought the place was a dump but it seemed to excite her. It shared its part of the beach with another hotel a few steps away that had a restaurant and a bar. She loved the idea of not having to drive anywhere to eat or have a drink. She would have all she needed. The sand and waves were extra.

I can't say that Tamma was preparing for her end because she seemed to continue her life with no noticeable change in routine. She still saw Bob and continued to drink too much. She packed up the things she wanted to keep and I helped her move to Pompano. Since she had been on her best behavior during the move I suggested we have dinner in Delray at her favorite restaurant, a wonderful Italian place on the beach. The food was great, I could get a properly prepared Caesar salad and they had a classical guitar artist who created a wonderful relaxed mood.

When we tried to walk in the door, I was stopped and told I was not welcome. They were refusing us service. I was furious. They wouldn't say why they just said you're not welcome here.

"We reserve the right to refuse service to anyone."

I'm a lawyer and understand the concept of "that depends." All facts are relevant. I grabbed the cop who was always on the street because of the Saturday crowds and asked him to help me find out why they were not letting me in a restaurant I regularly frequented.

The answer was that they had thrown Tamma and Bob out of the restaurant a few weeks before for drunken behavior. Bob had been particularly combative. When the doorman saw Tamma he assumed I was Bob even though I look nothing like Bob and in fact he had never

169

seen Bob. He just knew not to let that woman in, Tamma. What particularly annoyed me was that I was a regular patron and even knew the owner and his dad who lived in an apartment above the restaurant.

A few days later I went back for lunch, and sat at the bar with the owner and described the incident. He was very apologetic but told me the horror stories of trying to operate a fine restaurant in a beach area. The place was successful but he confessed he wished he was back in New York. He offered to buy me dinner but I said that wasn't necessary. The episode just reaffirmed that I had to distance myself from Tamma if she was not going to get help and I hoped to survive.

Tamma's body was changing from the alcohol damage. Her eyes had the yellow tint of jaundice and her waist was expanding as she retained fluid. Her mind was being altered. In lucid moments she would leave me notes like the ones above that ripped my heart apart. I felt completely helpless for the first time in my life. There were other notes and remarks that are too difficult to repeat or post.

Once at the beach in her modified hotel room she seemed happy and fell into a routine. What she learned shortly after the move was that the motel was being torn down to make way for something bigger and better. Tamma was "month to month" and would have to move again in four more months. I was paying Tamma's rent myself even after she had agreed to a marriage dissolution and I had given her a very generous settlement. I personally paid because Tamma would forget. Or more likely she used the money I gave her each month for drugs. The landlord was running a scam since the building was no longer licensed as a hotel and technically couldn't have guests. The good news was that he would never complain about Tamma or allow the police to visit.

Before Tamma moved she was once again rushed to the hospital. I was keeping her on my insurance so when she was admitted I got a call. At the time I was at least a half hour away but I raced to the hospital as quickly as possible. By now I ignored hospital rules and walked right into the room where she was being treated. They were

170

attempting to put an IV in her arm. Apparently she was filling the toilet bowl with blood before she arrived. It was not a hemorrhoid.

There seemed to be a bit of a frenzy in the hospital room. The resident and nurse were attempting to insert an IV in Tamma without much success. When I busted into the room Tamma had a smile for me and then told the intern in her command voice. "Put the IV in a vein near my groin." The resident was surprised but actually agreed and the nurse did as instructed. We were in a different hospital than before and the doctor was unknown to us. He was very gentle with Tamma and suggested she get on a liver transplant list. This was not the first time it was suggested and rejected by Tamma. After I left, a few hours later I was again contacted by the hospital because Tamma was asking to be discharged against medical advice. This was crazy and could also jeopardize the insurance reimbursement, but I was helpless to object and now legally divorced. She had a catheter inserted which she threatened to remove herself. After Tamma signed some papers they removed it and she was gone against medical advice. Apparently she took a cab home.

Sometime after this last event, I traveled to Cleveland for a family crisis that involved the court system and my youngest son. This trip was not a vacation, although it was wonderful to reconnect with some of my lifelong friends and of course say hello to Betsy. She asked me if I was going to my high school reunion. I had been unaware that it was being held Saturday night at a country club I belonged to years ago. It was a two night affair. The first night was at a hotel.

Unless you are starting to read this page before any of the others you know that high school was not my best experience. I had only gone to one other high school reunion and was always shocked at how many people were present who didn't look familiar. Since Betsy was in the class one year behind mine and was the star cheerleader, she knew many people in my class and wanted to go. Although she skipped Saturday night she joined me Friday.

One of my friends remarked a few years ago that he was always disappointed with reunions because the people he hoped to see didn't show up. Inevitably someone he wasn't interested in seeing would not only show up but grab him and never let go the entire evening. That had not been my experience, although I always did manage to find someone who couldn't wait to tell me all about their exciting life and achievements without thinking to ask a single question about mine.

Friday night I was having a good time and noticed a particularly attractive woman who I didn't remember from high school. I asked a friend who she was and the name Barbara connected, but she looked nothing like the girl I remembered who had an hourglass figure and was one of the few girls in our class who was a National Merit Scholar. I never spoke to her Friday night.

At the reunion on Saturday I saw her again and now after a few glasses of wine approached her, told her how beautiful I thought she was, and discovered she was in town to visit her mom. Barbara lived in California. I guess we were mutually attracted since we left together that night with promises to reunite.

In the next few months Barbara and I shuttled between West Palm Beach and Mountain View getting to know each other better. It had been so long since I had been physically intimate with a woman that I was discovering pleasures long since abandoned. The frequency of our calls and emails were becoming overwhelming and the three hour time difference made these personal exchanges a challenge.

Although we were no longer together Tamma was not happy with my travels. To avoid confrontation I told her I was in Belize but my phone rang constantly and with each call and lie, I became more depressed. I was lying to Tamma but also was not comfortable when I felt compelled to return her calls when I was with Barbara. Eventually Tamma somehow discovered the truth of my actual location and started calling Barbara and leaving disturbing messages. I told Barbara not to listen, but of course she digested every word and no doubt wondered how much of the rants was true.

And then the rants stopped. Tamma moved again after the forced closing of her beach hotel to a condo in Pompano Beach that seemed to suit her, mainly because Bob was now spending more time with her. I was happy for her although I knew this would probably mean even more physically destructive behavior. And in fact once again I received a call from Tamma's new landlord asking for help.

The condo was on the second floor of a building that looked like a motel except the rooms were much larger. All the rooms had a screened in back porch. Tamma's unit had two bicycles on the porch that apparently belonged to other condo owners. It appears Bob had "borrowed" them without bothering to return them and since they were clearly visible to anyone who looked at the porch from ground level, the owners wanted them back. Immediately. The landlord had not been able to reach Tamma and so contacted me since apparently Tamma had listed my name on her rental agreement. I agreed to meet the landlord although I told her Tamma and I were no longer married.

When I met the landlord at the condo I discovered a very nice Hispanic woman who was very distraught. I told her not to worry I would take the bikes out and return them to their owners.

"No that's not it. Come with me."

She directed me to the bathroom which looked like a murder scene. There was dried blood all over the floor. I had seen this before

173

and called Tamma to find out if she was okay. I reached her on her cell phone.

"I'm alright and being discharged today. They kept me two nights but I'll be back this afternoon."

I didn't bother to discuss the bikes and told her to call me later.

Before I hung up, I asked her about Bob.

"Is he living with you now?"

"Don't be silly. Bob is in jail. One too many DUI's."

I did my best to assure the landlord that the mess would be cleaned up. I blamed the bikes on a friend who was staying with her for a few days but was now gone to another state and she should not worry again. If there was a new problem contact me.

The following weekend, I walked the beach in Fort Lauderdale and had a long conversation with Barbara. This had become our routine while we struggled with trying to maintain a long distance relationship. After my walk I went to my favorite breakfast spot in Fort Lauderdale called The Floridian. They were a 24/7 restaurant that entertained some of the most colorful Fort Lauderdale residents. While I soaked up the remains of my eggs benedict, I remembered that they offered a great Thanksgiving prepared dinner that you could get to go. I thought about how I was going to manage to feed my mother and make sure Tamma didn't have to eat alone. The Floridian would be my solution.

Unfortunately the issue solved itself. Around 11am November 20, 2007, Bob called me in a panic. He said to come to Tamma's condo immediately, the police were there. Tamma is dead. His story was he had been released from jail, banged on the condo door, and when there was no response, broke the bathroom window and crawled through. He found Tamma on the side of the bed, blood on the floor and not responsive. He called 911 and the first responders confirmed that she was deceased. When they saw the broken window and Bob admitted he did not live there the police arrived. Bob called me to save himself from police interrogation about a possible murder.

During the 20 minute ride to the condo, Tamma's death did not register. My mind was blank. I arrived at the condo without awareness of the transit. It only took a few minutes to explain to the police my relationship to Tamma, her history and to confirm that although Bob was a drunk he was not a killer. They let Bob go. When I asked to see Tamma, they refused since I was no longer legally married to her and I was gently told to leave.

I stood in the parking lot with my eyes directed to the condo's door. I stood there over two hours, while I called the landlord and arranged for her to meet me and waited for the coroner to arrive. I watched while they rolled a cart out with a covered body of a 47 year old, bi-polar, possibly schizophrenic young woman who had been my wife and companion for over 20 years. The tears were a river building, and cresting towards a powerful dam, restraining their advance. A dam fortified from denial, acceptance and helplessness. Experiencing the death of someone you love was not new to me. Watching over a period of years someone you love killing herself in slow motion was unique. Could I have saved her?

When I finally cleared out the condo, I saw that Bob had rifled through her stuff, looking to grab whatever he could of value. Her wallet and purse were missing. I did find some of her costume jewelry hidden in her shoes. I threw all of her clothes into boxes, packed them as best I could to Fed Ex them to her sister, and then made arrangements for her cremation and ashes to be returned to a funeral home in Pompano Beach. When I took the boxes to FedEx, I was one of the first early morning customers. The woman behind the counter asked me to place the first box on the scale. As I struggled with the box, it began to fall apart. And I fell apart with the box. I struggled to hold back the tears. As I write this I am struggling once again to restrain them. The woman behind the counter without further comment started to prepare new boxes and began to repack all the contents. Over six boxes altogether. When I was able to control myself I explained to her the circumstances. She looked about Tamma's size and so I asked her if she wanted any of the many pair of jeans. She actually accepted some.

So moved by her kindness, a few weeks later I wrote FedEx about my experience in the hope that they would better appreciate one of their employees. They actually forwarded to me a copy of the letter they sent her applauding her kindness.

A few weeks later the ashes arrived. And not yet being able to verbalize my despair, I wrote about it.

It was a paper box that could have held a new router or portable clock radio. There was a wall of these boxes all the same size, as if one size fits all: a sumo wrestler or ballerina. On the cover of his box was an envelope addressed to the Memorial Company (Levitt-Weinstein) and the Certificate of Cremation for Tamma, done up like a prize. Inside the envelope another card Permit No. 422 signed by the Crematory.

He didn't want to open the box and didn't want to deal with the contents until he had thought it through, but then it was Tamma and he could imagine her saying: "What the hell is your problem?…Do this now! I'm not staying on the floor in your shitty filthy car. Put me in the ocean."

So he thought about where. Was there a boardwalk so the ashes wouldn't blow back on the beach? Did it matter? Were there rules about this stuff? Should he wait until it was dark? Say a special prayer?

He ended up on the beach in Delray by a restaurant called Luna Rosa because she loved to go there and they had spent most of their Florida time in Delray. It was raining now and so he just grabbed the box and dashed to the water and sat down on the sand and opened the box. He pulled out the clear, heavy plastic bag and dropped it in the sand between his legs.

The stuff inside (Tamma stuff) looked just like the sand but not as fine. It didn't look like ashes.

And then there was this plastic brad holding the bag together that clearly required a tool to safely remove. He could imagine a frustrated mourner just heaving the bag directly in the water or tearing the bag and having the ashes blow everywhere. So he worked the tab up the bag using his fingers like a needle nose pliers and somehow got it off.

He put his hand in the bag and let the ashes fall through his fingers. Inside the bag was a metal coin stamped ABCO Crematory 30336. With the bag open he walked into the ocean up to about his waist. He forgot that his wallet was still in his jeans. He let the ashes fall into a kind of milky cover, like creamer in your coffee.

He was alone with her.

She was not drunk.

No rabbi, no body in a box, no family.

Only one mourner.

There were other mourners in Cleveland, but I did not attend. Where were these people when I needed them? I did not feel they deserved to share my grief, and I was sure I would receive no comfort from them. My most immediate relief actually came from a Coldplay lyric: "Those who are dead are not dead, they're just living in my head." I was in the process of trying to rebuild Tamma to her former self, the girl I loved and the girl I married. My visits to my mother and attempt to build my relationship with Barbara slowed the process. I had not come to peace with my guilt and constant "what if" refrain. Could I have found more help for her, been more forceful? Why was she so resistant to help? I tried to find some relief again with words. So I wrote:

The waves and the beach were at war,
The wind watching in anticipation,
For she was there uninvited
Running naked and fearless on the sand:
A rude uninvited party guest.

He watched and then screamed:

"What do you think you're doing?"
The wind echoed: "Get out of here!"

Laughing, she dived headlong
Into the massive wave

that swallowed her

Like an angered great white

As it spit her to the surface
To be readied for the final
Massive salty bite.
The Onlooker locked her eyes

And her wink.

Did she not care because her mental condition and the noise in her brain made her life unlivable? I wished I could have asked God but that bit of succor was not available to me. I am not an atheist and probably not an agnostic. I am forever hopeful there is a compassionate loving force in the universe and maybe even a collective consciousness. But no one I've loved who has died has ever come back to visit, even in a dream. I'm waiting for Tamma to appear.

I visited for the first time in my life a psychologist who I called "my wise old man" because there was no bullshit about him. I was feeling guilty about meeting Barbara before Tamma had died. He had no great words of wisdom but began to remind me that I was human. Probably a difficult thing to grasp for someone who has been in codependent relationships most of his life.

During one of my more extended visits to Barbara I visited a psychologist in California, who said that it would take a long time to deal with my codependency, but maybe he had an answer to my post dramatic stress disorder. I had never thought of it that way before. He insisted that what I had endured with Tamma was comparable to battle fatigue. He suggested a new form of "light therapy." He called it EMDR or eye movement desensitization and reprocessing. This technique did not rely on "talk" but instead rapid eye movement guided by flashing lights while you relived your worst moments. I truly hope this works for some of our wounded soldiers. It had no effect

178

on me. My light therapy leader seemed happy to see me go since he was not getting a full reimbursement from my insurance company. He did suggest I get some future help for codependency.

Over the next few years after Tamma's death, I continued to wind down my work with the REIT. The quarterly meetings and sourcing work occupied me just enough to keep me sane. I took long motorcycle trips and wandered the beaches. I visited Belize often for Frank Speight until it became clear all was not right in his universe.

Frequent visits to Barbara were becoming difficult for me and troubling to Barbara. We were creating a new form of codependency. We were together but not really. A life is not a vacation, it is a complex series of day to day interactions. What we were play acting was not real life. After my mom died, I moved into her condo in Westin, Florida and tried to figure out what was next.

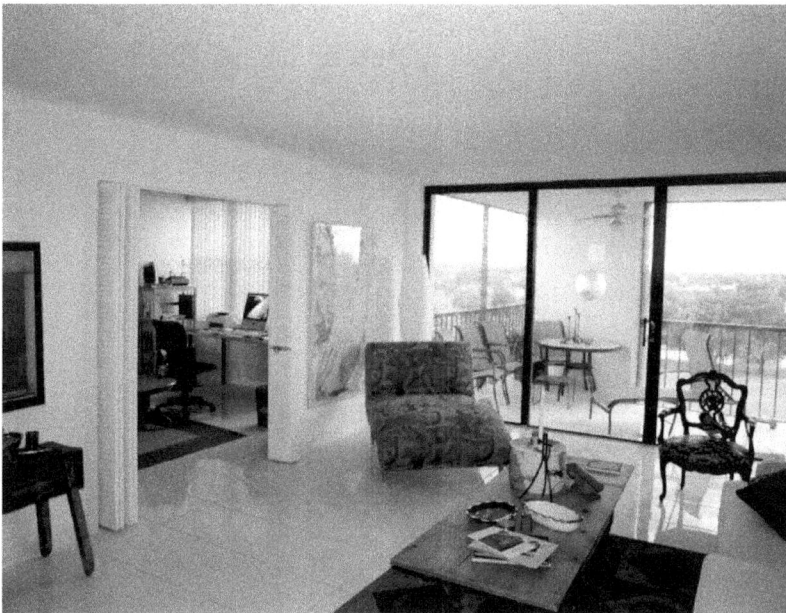

CHAPTER 16: WESTIN FLORIDA

IN ORDER FOR MY MOTHER to continue to live in her condo it was necessary to refinance her mortgage. Convincing my mother to sign the necessary documents was not an easy task. Although I probably could have executed the documents using my durable power of attorney, my mother still had capacity, and I was not willing to avoid the discussion with her about money. She relented and we used the money to settle up the bills and much of my father's debt.

After my mother's death, I moved into the condo and began a long necessary remodel project. The plastic kitchen ceiling was now replaced with modern lighting. The counters all altered as well as the appliances modernized. The tub in the master bathroom was removed and converted into a walk in shower. The furniture was removed and replaced. The old stuff was all donated to a church along with my parents clothing. We saved a few items. My mother's mink coat that no one wanted still hangs in the closet, but all the silver plated stuff was thrown away.

Both my kids have been divorced and remarried and both have their own children. So I am a grandfather but one with a little less status than my grandfathers had. Kids today may have three or four sets of living grandparents. No one in my youth spoke of "step grandparents" but it is what it is. On the plus side, we didn't have Skype and essentially free telephones in the 50's. My kids used to hang on for their lives without a helmet on the luggage rack of my English racer. They would slide beltless side to side in the back seat of our Chevy as we speeded along. They sat alone locked in the car as we ran into 7 Eleven for milk and they were not expected to know much as kids. We were not shamed into buying expensive toys that would give them an edge in kindergarten. They heard the Stones, not Mozart. We had cloth diapers and a diaper man not paper diapers with Velcro.

The first time I had an opportunity to spend some real time with my granddaughter, we were at a hotel swimming pool where my divorced son was doing his "visit." My granddaughter was enjoying jumping into my arms in the pool over and over. Finally after about the tenth jump she looked at me and asked: "What did you say your name was?" I was saddened and delighted at the same time.

At Westin I was getting to know my little grandson. There is a special bond when you get to sleep alone with a toddler. I loved to lay inches from his sleeping head and watch and listen to him breathe. That wonderful careless sleep and porcelain skin. Is there a better blessing in the world than a healthy child? And is there a better sound than a child's laughter?

I went back to work and spent a few days a week as corporate counsel for a lens coating company. I was a lawyer and papa to a young company. I was underpaid and underappreciated, but at least it was something to do. When the REIT was sold I had a large payday and felt safe taking a chance on moving to California. Before the move, I had an experience in Washington, DC I will never forget.

OMAHA, Neb.--(BUSINESS WIRE)--**Government Properties Trust, Inc. (NYSE: GPT)** ("GPT"), a self-managed, self-administered real estate investment trust, and Record Realty Trust (ASX: RRT) ("Record Realty"), an Australian listed property trust today announced that they have entered into a definitive merger agreement whereby a subsidiary of Record Realty will acquire GPT for $10.75 per common share in cash, subject to a potential reduction by an amount not to exceed $0.08 per common share resulting from certain potential contingencies of GPT, and as otherwise provided in the merger agreement.

The transaction resulted in large fees for institutions involved. One of them was anxious to reward the board members of GPT. We were all invited to Washington, D.C. for a final dinner to celebrate. The party was held at the Mandarin Oriental Hotel Saturday evening. Since the hotel was walking distance to the Holocaust Museum I decided to visit. I had never been there before. Two things in the incredible museum particularly moved me. The first was the number of newsreels from the period, which highlighted just how insensitive Americans were to the blight of the Jews. The second and most moving to me was an actual railcar used for deportation of Jews to the camps. The number of people packed into the cars sickened me. I wrote a poem about it almost immediately afterward:

Railcar Moment

Track ripped from Treblinka balances
The mystical box car from Poland;
Once a 15ton transport to Genocide
Now restored to play another role.

Not 100 or more crushed lives
A trip; but two million a year
Travel sucked through a black hole
Of grief and screams, with just a few steps,
To be warned by souls still stirring:

That humanities train wrecks
Are not stalled cars on the freeway,
Slowing a trip to the bye and bye,
But massive strokes; conscience coronaries
That could cause our final solution.

And to Jews who enjoyed Bar mitzvah;
Sans tattoo number on arm;
Do not forget the Railcar Moment.
The next may not be a day
At the museum.

Stunned from the experience, I returned to the hotel and got ready for the evening extravagance. I dressed in my best suit and met the other board members in the lobby for our first round of cocktails before the dinner.

After several more drinks Barack Obama not yet officially a candidate for President entered the lounge area of the lobby and approached several tables for a meet and greet. He did not approach ours. I was already an Obama fan after reading an article in the New

182

Yorker that told the story of how he had become Chairman of the Harvard Law Review as a law student there. I knew the politics involved with that achievement and was fascinated by his ability to mediate differences and still be liked.

All sense of propriety having been overcome by the effects of alcohol, I decided to get up and chase after our future President as he retreated from the lobby of the Mandarin. As he was about to exit accompanied by only one friend, I put both hands on his shoulders and stopped him long enough to probably be his worst nightmare of the day.

"Hello, you didn't stop by our table but I wanted to say I am a huge admirer. I'm from Ohio and now living in Florida, two very important states for you if you run. I hope I can help."

Stunned but gracious he said: "Thank you very much."

I didn't realize until much later what an ass I had been and today realize that similar conduct would have gotten me shot.

Later that evening our party was held in a private area of the hotel reserved for events like ours. There was a small bar area before the entrance to our reserved room where our future President and his wife sat enjoying conversation and a cocktail. I wanted to stop and apologize but I thought the best approach was to sneak by and say nothing.

Barbara's and my relationship would not survive if we didn't move in together. But forever cautious, I was not ready to abandon my Westin residence. Living together is different from dating, particularly dating long distance. I wanted to keep Westin available if things didn't work out. Before the move I pursued a new hobby.

I love ITunes U and YouTube. Lifelong learning is my mantra and so one day when I thought it would be fun to paint, I went to YouTube to watch other people do it. I thought if I learned too much, it would take the fun out of it so I just jumped right in. I had no idea what to expect but knew it would be fun to push paint around on a canvas. I chose acrylics because they were cheaper and easier to clean up. I painted in the bathroom with the canvas on the floor. Why not. The cover of this book was one of my first paintings.

And then suddenly I was living in California. It is difficult to live in someone else's house. You are surrounded with a collection of things that may or may not please you. I am always redecorating everything I see including people. Barbara's house was decorated in a style not my own although it was comfortable and beautiful and of course, a representation of the books, music and art that were important to her. She had lived in the house since the mid 80's. Her walls were filled with amazing Inuit art and her CD collection was complete with the best of classical and jazz. Her books were arranged in a patterned manner as only a former librarian could accomplish. But I am not ordered and arranged and I am most represented by a clash of contrasting primary colors so settling into this new environment was going to be a challenge.

Mountain View, California is the home of Google and is located in the heart of Silicon Valley. The demographics are far different from Florida or Ohio. There are over 20 languages spoken on the streets in downtown Mountain View and some of the most brilliant math and science young people in the world walk its streets. They are also very well paid and privileged by circumstances.

I am sure there are brilliant accountants and attorneys in other parts of the country who cannot find employment because the profession and hometown they chose has been altered by technology to their detriment. By contrast, there are not enough trained programmers and engineers to fill the hunger of the Silicon Valley.

I was trying very hard to be a Californian. I had my car shipped out with a little of what was left of the Florida things that I felt I couldn't leave behind. Only what could fit in my car. I was prepared to begin fresh and was committed to call Florida yesterday's story.

But I was not over Tamma's death. There had been no real closure. I had not been properly comforted by friends, I had not attended a funeral and I was still feeling guilt. Barbara did all she could to make me comfortable but I was not ready. I found innocent things she did suddenly irritating and I'm sure she was often disappointed by my attitude. So my brief experiment ended and after a few short months. Once again my car sat filled with things on a large truck on a one way trip to Westin, Florida.

After I returned I spent months unraveling the mess Frank Speight had created in Belize and tried to recapture funds for one of his frauds that had involved some of my investors. I spent some time in Cleveland and renewed some friendships that I had let wane. But I missed Barbara.

And Barbara missed me.

CHAPTER 17: BARBARA: CALIFORNIA

WE DECIDED TO TRY AGAIN. I confirmed my commitment by renting the Westin condo furnished. There was no safety net now for at least the term of the new tenant's lease. It seemed easier now to leave the East Coast behind. So many of the important people in my life out east were now deceased. I was the last one standing in my core family and some of my best friends were also gone. My youngest son was in Cleveland but like the reality of divorced families everywhere in the new jet age, his children were in Nevada. My oldest son had very young children in Florida but he lived in an airplane because of business and I knew I would see him often. Whatever was left of my career in real estate and private placements seemed to no longer interest me. The new crowdfunding securities law opened up a future for online fund raising and I created one of the earliest attempts to educate owners and developers about this opportunity. But like an aging race horse, the truth was I just wanted to be put out to pasture.

I became fascinated with the potential of the world of online communications. Skype and later Zoom offer unlimited possibilities to bring people together to share ideas and also to resolve disputes. I had become certified as a mediator in Florida and began mediation services in California, but I dreamed of the potential to resolve disputes online and created a website where you could meet online with a mediator to settle disputes. I also saw this as a vehicle to have family meetings online to resolve family issues. I focused on helping families deal with the new challenge of their elderly parents' needs. Barbara spent her time focusing on the challenges of weight loss. Having successfully survived a serious eating disorder she followed her passion by becoming a leader and coach with Weight Watchers.

The challenges of living with and understanding someone much younger no longer existed with Barbara. I understood her physical aches and pains and she understood mine. We were two completed entities sharing our lives. This was not a codependent relationship.

Barbara worked in the Silicon Valley for a high tech pioneer before the incredible developments of the Valley were well known. She used her Mensa brain and library skills to become an expert high tech writer. Her skills at the piano reintroduced me to the joys of classical music, and we became weekend hikers exploring the many parks the area has to offer. Frequent trips to San Francisco exposed me to incredible art, the mysteries of Chinatown and the charm of a city that had sparked a cultural revolution in the 60's.

Before I met Barbara, my travel plans had been limited to the Caribbean and Canada. That was about to change. Barbara had the travel bug and had already seen much of the world. My kids had been to Europe. Steven spent his senior year of college in London. I had never been to Europe. So after exploring with Barbara most of what the miraculous California had to offer, including Yosemite and the redwoods, we visited London and Paris together and later Viet Nam, Portland and most of New Mexico. If we stay healthy we will be going on a four month cruise around the world early next year.

I spend my volunteer time as a field ombudsman advocating for seniors in assisted living facilities, memory care facilities and skilled nursing facilities licensed by the State of California. After meeting some amazing seniors, I started a podcast called The Reluctant Senior on iTunes. I am still painting and writing poetry.

I am comforted by my sons' parenting skills and for the fact that they draw comfort from their brotherly love. I am proud of their accomplishments but most proud of the way they have handled adversity. My grandchildren have been blessed with healthy bodies and strong intellect. I believe they will thrive in this very difficult fast changing world. We were all together for my 70th birthday in Cleveland.

Chapter 18: What's it all about?

YOU WOULD THINK THAT WHEN YOU REACH YOUR 70'S you would have a better understanding of yourself. And that understanding would help you unravel the predominant patterns of your life by employing a more mature analysis and review. Maybe. Yet even now I am not sure I can determine the difference between behavior that qualifies as codependent and behavior that is just an exuberant display of love.

I know the dynamics of my early childhood home profoundly affected my relationships and motivations. But I also believe some of us have a greater capacity for empathy than others. My grandfather cried every night during the news, both for the sad stories and the uplifting ones. I inherited the cry gene.

The longer I stay alive and interact with the glow and flow of existence, the more I appreciate the complexity and mystery of our lives. We live in an unknown environment. The bulk of the universe consists of dark energy (73%) and dark matter (23%) neither of which has been identified. All the stars and planets are only 4%. No one has yet explained consciousness. My grandson wants to be an astrophysicist. Maybe he will figure it all out.

I think I have survived cancer (it's an ongoing watch) and I still can enjoy most activities that require an operating body but my days of existence are limited. I am mortal. Recent discussions about the future of AI have made some suggest that humans will always be unique because they have an enduring soul. Okay. I have never spent much time wondering about the existence of God. Am I afraid I am going to HELL?

Do I hope to go to HEAVEN? Will I be chanting OM near the end?

I saw my mother exactly five minutes before she died and immediately afterwards. The difference was striking and indescribable. Without that thing that is life, the body is just a piece of flesh. Dispose of it as you will. With or without prayers. One of the things that fascinated me about Jewish prayers that mention God is that they never say the Hebrew word for God but instead use a code word. The idea is that the mere word itself is too holy to be spoken. And maybe too mysterious.

My God is that mysterious. So beyond explanation that I have not yet found a religion to warrant his mystery or complexity.

So what's it all about? I think it's about learning to love yourself or at least accept yourself. All of us were blessed with a spot of life on the planet. Who is to say we are not worthy. Everyone has their very own pile of problems. Be careful who you want to change places with. I cherish my relationships with old and new friends. I am blessed to be able to communicate with my grandchildren and learn from them. I feel real love and believe I am capable of returning love.

I used to relate to the scene in my favorite movie "All That Jazz," where Roy Scheider acting as Bob Fosse splashes water in his face, looks at his weary face and bloodshot eyes in the mirror, and says to the mirror: "It's show time, folks." Now each morning I squeegee, the shower door, and think, "Didn't I just do this minutes ago. Could it already be another day?" The days are moving faster now. I need to hold on to each a little longer.

I hope I have finally learned that I am only human. It's hard enough to repair myself much less try to fix someone else. I will probably second guess my past behavior for the rest of my life but I will do so now with acceptance of the imperfect logic of the human heart.

ABOUT THE AUTHOR

In addition to practicing law for over 40 years, Richard H. Schwachter, has been a real estate developer, a founding board member of a NYSE REIT, a principal of a securities broker dealership, a Series 7 broker, a mediator and an ombudsman. He is a graduate of Case Western Reserve Law School and the University of Wisconsin, cum laude. He is an author and an artist and a proud grandfather of five.

www.ingramcontent.com/pod-product-compliance
Lightning Source LLC
Chambersburg PA
CBHW070957040426
42443CB00007B/551